Essentials of Classic Italian Cooking

Italian Dishes Made for the Modern Kitchen

By
Urbano De Luca

Essentials of Classic Italian Cooking

Contents

Sauces

- Soups 9
- Minestre 15
- Fish 17
- Beef, Mutton, Veal, Lamb. 28
- Tongue, Sweetbread, Calf's Head, Liver, Suckling Pig 36
- Fowl, Duck, Game, Hare, Rabbit. 51
- Vegetables 60
- Macaroni, Rice, Polenta, and Other Italian Pastes 69
- Omelettes And Other Egg Dishes 75
- Sweets and Cakes 79

By Urbano De Luca

Essentials of Classic Italian Cooking

By Urbano De Luca

SAUCES

No. 1. Espagnole, or Brown Sauce

The chief ingredient of this useful sauce is good stock, to which add any remnants and bones of fowl or game. Butter the bottom of a stewpan with at least two ounces of butter, and in it put slices of lean veal, ham, bacon, cuttings of beef, fowl, or game trimmings, three peppercorns, mushroom trimmings, a tomato, a carrot and a turnip cut up, an onion stuck with two cloves, a bay leaf, a sprig of thyme, parsley and marjoram. Put the lid on the stewpan and braize well for fifteen minutes, then stir in a tablespoonful of flour, and pour in a quarter pint of good boiling stock and boil very gently for fifteen minutes, then strain through a tamis, skim off all the grease, pour the sauce into an earthenware vessel, and let it get cold. If it is not rich enough, add a little Liebig or glaze. Pass through a sieve again before using.

No. 2. Velute Sauce

The same as above, but use white stock, no beef, and only pheasant or fowl trimmings, button mushrooms, cream instead of glaze, and a chopped shallot.

No. 3. Bechamel Sauce

Ingredients: Butter, ham, veal, carrots, shallot, celery bay leaf, cloves, thyme, peppercorns, potato flour, cream, fowl stock.

Prepare a mirepoix by mixing two ounces of butter, trimmings of lean veal and ham, a carrot, a shallot, a little celery, all cut into dice, a bay leaf, two cloves, four peppercorns, and a little thyme. Put this on a moderate fire so as not to let it colour, and when all the moisture is absorbed add a tablespoonful of potato flour. Mix well, and gradually add equal quantities of cream and fowl stock, and stir till it boils. Then let it simmer gently. Stir occasionally, and if it gets too thick, add more cream and white stock. After two hours pass it twice slowly through a tamis so as to get the sauce very smooth.

No. 4. Mirepoix Sauce (for masking)

Ingredients: Bacon, onions, carrots, ham, a bunch of herbs, parsley, mushrooms, cloves, peppercorns, stock, Chablis.

Put the following ingredients into a stewpan: Some bits of bacon and lean ham, a carrot, all cut into dice, half an onion, a bunch of herbs, a few mushroom cuttings, two cloves, and four peppercorns. To this add one and a quarter pint of good stock and a glass of Chablis, boil rapidly for ten minutes then simmer till it is reduced to a third. Pass through a sieve and use for masking meat, fowl, fish, &c.

No. 5. Genoese Sauce

Ingredients: Onion, butter, Burgundy, mushrooms, truffles, parsley, bay leaf, Espagnole sauce (No.1), blond of veal, essence of fish, anchovy butter, crayfish or lobster butter.

Cut up a small onion and fry it in butter, add a glass of Burgundy, some cuttings of mushrooms and truffles, a pinch of chopped parsley and half a bay leaf. Reduce half. In another saucepan put two cups of Espagnole sauce, one cup of veal stock, and a tablespoonful of essence of fish, reduce one-third and add it to the other saucepan, skim off all the grease, boil for a few minutes, and pass through a sieve. Then stir it over the fire, and add half a teaspoonful of crayfish and half of anchovy butter.

No. 6. Italian Sauce

Ingredients: Chablis, mushrooms, leeks, a bunch of herbs, peppercorns, Espagnole sauce, game gravy or stock, lemon.

Put into a stewpan two glasses of Chablis, two tablespoonsful of mushroom trimmings, a leek cut up, a bunch of herbs, five peppercorns, and boil till it is reduced to half. In another stewpan mix two glasses of Espagnole (No. 1) or Velute sauce (No 2) and half a glass of game gravy, boil for a few minutes then blend the contents of the two stewpans, pass through a sieve, and add the juice of a lemon.

No. 7. Ham Sauce, Salsa di Prosciutto

Ingredients: Ham, Musca or sweet port, vinegar, basil spice.

Cut up an ounce of ham and pound it in a mortar then mix it with three dessert spoonsful of port or Musca and a teaspoonful of vinegar a little dried basil and a pinch of spice. Boil it up, and then pass it through a sieve and warm it up in a bain-marie. Serve with roast meats. If you cannot get a sweet wine add half a teaspoonful of sugar. Australian Muscat is a good wine to use.

No. 8. Tarragon Sauce

Ingredients: Tarragon, stock, butter, flour.

To half a pint of good stock add two good sprays of fresh tarragon, simmer for quarter of an hour in a stewpan and keep the lid on. In another stewpan melt one ounce of butter and mix it with three dessert-spoonsful of flour, then gradually pour the stock from the first stewpan over it, but take out the tarragon. Mix well, add a teaspoonful of finely chopped tarragon and boil for two minutes.

No. 9. Tomato Sauce

Ingredients: Tomatoes, ham, onions, basil, salt, oil, garlic, spices.

Broil three tomatoes, skin them and mix them with a tablespoonful of chopped ham, half an onion, salt, a dessert-spoonful of oil, a little pounded spice and basil. Then boil and pass through a sieve. Whilst the sauce is boiling, put in a clove of garlic with a cut, but remove it before you pass the sauce through the sieve.

No. 10. Tomato Sauce Piquante

Ingredients: Ham, butter, onion, carrot, celery, bay leaf, thyme, cloves, peppercorns, vinegar, Chablis, stock, tomatoes, Velute or Espagnole sauce, castor sugar, lemon.

Cut up an ounce of ham, half an onion, half a carrot, half a stick of celery very fine, and fry them in butter together with a bay leaf, a sprig of thyme, one clove and four peppercorns. Over this pour a third of a cup of vinegar, and when the liquid is all absorbed, add half a glass of Chablis and a cup of stock. Then add six tomatoes cut up and strained of all their liquid. Cook this in a covered stewpan and pass it through a sieve, but see that none of the bay leaf or thyme goes through. Mix this sauce with an equal quantity of Velute (No. 2) or Espagnole sauce, (No. 1), let it boil and pass through a sieve again and at the last add a teaspoonful of castor sugar, the juice of half a lemon, and an ounce of fresh butter. (Another tomato sauce may be made like this, but use stock instead of vinegar and leave out the lemon juice and sugar.)

No. 11. Mushroom Sauce

Ingredients: Velute sauce, essence of mushrooms, butter.

Mix two dessert-spoonsful of essence of mushrooms with a cupful of Velute sauce (No. 2), reduce, keep on stirring, and just before serving add an ounce of butter. This sauce can be made with essence of truffle, or game, or shallot.

No. 12. Neapolitan Sauce

Ingredients: Onions, ham, butter, Marsala, blond of veal, thyme, bay leaf, peppercorns, cloves, mushrooms, Espagnole sauce (No. 1), tomato sauce, game stock or essence.

Fry an onion in butter with some bits of cut-up ham, then pour a glass of Marsala over it, and another of blond of veal, add a sprig of thyme, a bay leaf, four peppercorns, a clove, a tablespoonful of mushroom cuttings, and reduce half. In another saucepan put two cups of Espagnole sauce, one cupful of tomato sauce, and half a cup of game stock or essence. Reduce a third, and add the contents of the first saucepan, boil the sauce a few minutes, and pass it through a sieve. Warm it up in a bain-marie before using.

No. 13. Neapolitan Anchovy Sauce

Ingredients: Anchovies, fennel, flour, spices, parsley, marjoram, garlic, lemon juice, vinegar, cream.

Wash three anchovies in vinegar, bone and pound them in a mortar with a teaspoonful of chopped fennel and a pinch of cinnamon. Then mix in a teaspoonful of chopped parsley and marjoram, a squeeze of lemon juice, a teaspoonful of flour, half a gill of boiled cream and the bones of the fish for which you will use this sauce. Pass through a sieve, add a clove of garlic with a cut in it, and boil. If the fish you are using is cooked in the oven, add a little of the liquor in which it has been cooked to the sauce. Take out the garlic before serving. Instead of anchovies you may use caviar, pickled tunny, or any other pickled fish.

No. 14. Roman Sauce (Salsa Agro-dolce)

Ingredients: Espagnole sauce, stock, burnt sugar, vinegar, raisins, pine nuts or almonds.

Mix two spoonsful of burnt sugar with one of vinegar, and dilute with a little good stock. Then add two cups of Espagnole sauce (No. 1), a few stoned raisins, and a few pinocchi* (pine nuts) or shredded almonds. Keep this hot in a bain-marie, and serve with cutlets, calf's head or feet or tongue.

*The pinocchi which Italians use instead of almonds can be bought when in season.

No. 15. Roman Sauce (another way)

Ingredients: Espagnole sauce, an onion, butter, flour, lemon, herbs, nutmeg, raisins, pine nuts or almonds, burnt sugar.

Cut up a small bit of onion, fry it slightly in butter and a little flour, add the juice of a lemon and a little of the peel grated, a bouquet of herbs, a pinch of nutmeg, a few stoned raisins, shredded almonds or pinocchi, and a tablespoonful of burnt sugar. Add this to a good Espagnole (No. 1), and warm it up in a bain-marie.

No. 16. Supreme Sauce

Ingredients: White sauce, fowl stock, butter.

Put three-quarters of a pint of white sauce into a saucepan, and when it is nearly boiling add half a cup of concentrated fowl stock. Reduce until the sauce is quite thick, and when about to serve pass it through a tamis into a bain-marie and add two tablespoonsful of cream.

No. 17. Pasta marinate (For masking Italian Frys)

Ingredients: Semolina flour, eggs, salt, butter (or olive oil), vinegar, water.

Mix the following ingredients well together: two ounces of semolina flour, the yolks of two eggs, a little salt, and two ounces of melted butter. Add a glass of water so as to form a liquid substance. At the last add the whites of two eggs beaten up to a snow. This will make a good paste for masking meat, fish, vegetables, or sweets which are to be fried in the Italian manner, but if for meat or vegetables add a few drops of vinegar or a little lemon juice.

No. 18. White Villeroy

Ingredients: Butter, flour, eggs, cream, nutmeg, white stock.

Make a light-coloured roux by frying two ounces of butter and two ounces of flour, stir in some white stock and keep it very smooth. Let it boil, and add the yolks of three eggs, mixed with two tablespoonsful of cream and a pinch of nutmeg. Pass it through a sieve and use for masking cutlets, fish, &c.

SOUPS

No. 19. Clear Soup

Ingredients: Stock meat, water, a bunch of herbs (thyme, parsley, chervil, bay leaf, basil, marjoram), three carrots, three turnips, three onions, three cloves stuck in the onions, one blade of mace.

Cut up three pounds of stock meat small and put it in a stock pot with two quarts of cold water, three carrots, and three turnips cut up, three onions with a clove stuck in each one, a bunch of herbs and a blade of mace. Let it come to the boil and then draw it off, at once skim off all the scum, and keep it gently simmering, and occasionally add two or three tablespoonsful of cold water. Let it simmer all day, and then strain it through a fine cloth.

Some of the liquor in which a calf's head has been cooked, or even a calf's foot, will greatly improve a clear soup.

The stock should never be allowed to boil as long as the meat and vegetables are in the stock pot.

No. 20. Zuppa Primaverile (Spring Soup)

Ingredients: Clear soup, vegetables.

Any fresh spring vegetables will do for this soup, but they must all be cooked separately and put into the soup at the last minute. It is best made with fresh peas, asparagus tips, and a few strips of tarragon.

No. 21. Soup alla Lombarda

Ingredients: Clear soup, fowl forcemeat, Bechamel (No. 3), peas, lobster butter, eggs, asparagus.

Make a firm forcemeat of fowl and divide it into three parts, to the first add two spoonsful of cream Bechamel, to the second four spoonsful of puree of green peas, to the third two spoonsful of lobster butter and the yolk of an egg; thus you will have the Italian colours, red, white, and green. Butter a pie dish and make little quenelles of the forcemeat. Just before serving boil them for four minutes in boiling stock, take them out carefully and put them in a warm soup tureen with two spoonsful of cooked green peas and pour a very fresh clear soup over them. Hand little croutons fried in lobster butter separately.

No. 22. Tuscan Soup

Ingredients: Stock, eggs.

Whip up three or four eggs, gradually add good stock to them, and keep on whisking them up until they begin to curdle. Keep the soup hot in a bain-marie.

No. 23. Venetian Soup

Ingredients: Clear soup, butter, flour, Parmesan, eggs.

Make a roux by frying two ounces of butter and two ounces of flour, add an ounce of grated cheese and half a cup of good stock. Mix up well so as to form a paste, and then take it off the fire and add the yolks of four eggs, mix again and form the again and form the paste into little quenelles. Boil these in a little soup, strain off, put them into the tureen and pour a good clear soup over them.

No. 24. Roman Soup

Ingredients: Stock, butter, eggs, salt, crumb of bread, parsley, nutmeg, flour, Parmesan.

Mix three and a half ounces of butter with two eggs and four ounces of crumbs of bread soaked in stock, a little chopped parsley, salt, and a pinch of nutmeg. Reduce this and add two tablespoonsful of flour and one of grated Parmesan. Form this into little quenelles and boil them in stock for a few minutes put them into a tureen and pour a good clear soup over them.

No. 25. Soup alla Nazionale

Ingredients: Clear soup, savoury custard.

Make a savoury custard and divide it into three parts, one to be left white, another coloured red with tomato, and the third green with spinach. Put a layer of each in a buttered saucepan and cook for about ten minutes, cut it into dice, so that you have the three Italian colours (red, white, and green) together, then put the custard into a soup tureen and pour a good clear soup over it.

No. 26. Soup alla Modanese

Ingredients: Stock, spinach, butter, salt, eggs, Parmesan, nutmeg, croutons.

Wash one pound of spinach in five or six waters, then chop it very fine and mix it with three ounces of butter, salt it and warm it up. Then let it get cold, pass through a hair sieve, and add two eggs, a tablespoonful of grated Parmesan, and very little nutmeg. Add this to some boiling stock in a copper saucepan, put on the lid, and on the top put some hot coals so that the eggs may curdle and help to thicken the soup. Serve with fried croutons.

No. 27. Crotopo Soup

Ingredients: Clear soup, veal, ham, eggs, salt, pepper, nutmeg, rolls.

Pound half a pound of lean veal in a mortar, then add three ounces of cooked ham with some fat in it, the yolk of an egg, salt, pepper, and very little nutmeg. Pass through a sieve, cut some small French rolls into slices, spread them with the above mixture, and colour them in the oven. Then cut them in halves or quarters, put them into a tureen, and just before serving pour a very good clear soup over them.

No. 28. Soup all'Imperatrice

Ingredients: Breast of fowl, eggs, salt, pepper, ground rice, nutmeg, clear stock.

Pound the breast of a fowl in a mortar, and add to it a teaspoonful of ground rice, the yolk of an egg, salt, pepper, and a pinch of nutmeg. Pass this through a sieve, form quenelles with it, and pour a good clear soup over them.

No. 29. Neapolitan Soup

Ingredients: Fowl, potato flour, eggs, Bechamel sauce, peas, asparagus, spinach, clear soup.

Mix a quarter pound of forcemeat of fowl with a tablespoonful of potato flour, a tablespoonful of Bechamel sauce (No. 3), and the yolk of an egg; put this into a tube about the size round of an ordinary macaroni; twenty minutes before serving squirt the forcemeat into a saucepan with boiling stock, and nip off the forcemeat as it comes through the pipe into pieces about an inch and a half long. Let it simmer, and add boiled peas and asparagus tips. If you like to have the fowl macaroni white and green, you can colour half the forcemeat with a spoonful of spinach colouring. Serve in a good clear soup.

No. 30. Soup with Risotto

Ingredients: Risotto (No. 189), eggs, bread crumbs, clear or brown soup.

If you have some good risotto left, you can use it up by making it into little balls the size of small nuts. Egg and bread crumb and fry them in butter; dry them and put them into a soup tureen with hot soup. The soup may be either clear or brown.

No. 31. Soup alla Canavese

Ingredients: White stock, butter, onions, carrot, celery, tomato, cauliflower, fat bacon, parsley, sage, Parmesan, salt, pepper.

Chop up half an onion, half a carrot, half a stick of celery, a small bit of fat bacon, and fry them in two ounces of butter. Then cover them with good white stock, boil for a few minutes, pass through a sieve, and add two tablespoonsful of tomato puree. Then blanch half a cauliflower in salted water, let it get cold, drain all the water out of it, and break it up into little bunches and put them into a stock pot with the stock, a small leaf of dried sage, crumbled up, and a little chopped parsley, and let it all boil; add a pinch of grated cheese and some pepper. Serve with grated Parmesan handed separately.

No. 32. Soup alla Maria Pia

Ingredients: White stock, eggs, butter, peas, white beans, carrot, onion, leeks, celery, cream croutons.

Soak one pound of white beans for twelve hours, then put them into a stock pot with a little salt, butter, and water, add a carrot, an onion, two leeks, and a stick of celery, and simmer until the vegetables are well cooked; then take out all the fresh vegetables, drain the beans and pass them through a sieve, but first dilute them with good stock. Put this puree into a stock pot with good white stock, and when it has boiled keep it hot in a bain-marie until you are about to serve; then mix the yolk of three eggs in a cup of cream, and add this to the soup. Pour the soup into a warm tureen, add some boiled green peas, and serve with fried croutons handed separately.

No. 33. Zuppa d' Erbe (Lettuce Soup)

Ingredients: Stock, sorrel, endive, lettuce, chervil, celery, carrot, onion, French roll, Parmesan cheese.

Boil the following vegetables and herbs in very good stock for an hour: Two small bunches of sorrel, a bunch of endive, a lettuce, a small bunch of chervil, a stick of celery, a carrot and an onion, all well washed and cut up. Then put some slices of toasted French roll into a tureen and pour the above soup over them. Serve with grated Parmesan handed separately.

No. 34. Zuppa Regina di Riso (Queen's Soup)

Ingredients: Fowl stock, ground rice, milk, butter.

Put a tablespoonful of ground rice into a saucepan and gradually add half a pint of milk, boil it gently for twelve minutes in a bainmarie, but stir the whole time, so as to get it very smooth. Just before serving add an ounce of butter, pass it through a sieve, and mix it with good fowl stock.

MINESTRE

Minestra is a thick broth, very much like hotch-potch, only thicker. In Italy it is often served at the beginning of dinner instead of soup; it also makes an excellent lunch dish. Two or three tablespoonsful of No. 35 will be found a great improvement to any of these minestre.

No. 35. A Condiment for Seasoning Minestre, &c.

Ingredients: Onions, celery, carrots, butter, salt, stock, tomatoes, mushrooms.

Cut up an onion, a stick of celery, and a carrot; fry them in butter and salt; add a few bits of cooked ham and veal cut up, two mushrooms, and the pulp of a tomato. Cook for a quarter of an hour, and add a little stock occasionally to keep it moist. Pass through a sieve, and use for seasoning minestre, macaroni, rice, &c. It should be added when the dish is nearly cooked.

No. 36. Minestra alla Casalinga

Ingredients: Rice, butter, stock, vegetables.

All sorts of vegetables will serve for this dish. Blanch them in boiling salted water, then drain and fry them in butter. Add plenty of good stock, and put them on a slow fire. Boil four ounces of rice in stock, and when it is well done add the stock with the vegetables. Season with two or three spoonsful of No. 35, and serve with grated cheese handed separately.

No. 37. Minestra of Rice and Turnips

Ingredients: Rice, turnips, butter, gravy, tomatoes.

Cut three or four young turnips into slices and put them on a dish, strew a little salt over them, cover them with another dish, and let them stand for about two hours until the water has run out of them. Then drain the slices, put them in a frying-pan and fry them slightly in butter. Add some good gravy and mashed-up tomatoes, and after having cooked this for a few minutes pour it into good boiling stock. Add three ounces of well-washed rice, and boil for half-an-hour.

Minestra loses its flavour if it is boiled too long. In Lombardy, however, rice, macaroni, &c., are rarely boiled enough for English tastes.

No. 38. Minestra alla Capucina

Ingredients: Rice, anchovies, butter, stock, and onions.

Scale an anchovy, pound it, and fry it in butter together with a small onion cut across, and four ounces of boiled rice. Add a little salt, and when the rice is a golden brown, take out the onion and gradually add some good stock until the dish is of the consistency of rice pudding.

No. 39. Minestra of Semolina

Ingredients: Stock, semolina, Parmesan.

Put as much stock as you require into a saucepan, and when it begins to boil add semolina very gradually, and stir to keep it from getting lumpy Cook it until the semolina is soft, and serve with grated Parmesan handed separately. To one quart of soup use three ounces of semolina.

No. 40. Minestrone alla Milanese

Ingredients: Rice or macaroni, ham, bacon, stock, all sorts of vegetables.

Minestrone is a favourite dish in Lombardy when vegetables are plentiful. Boil all sorts of vegetables in stock, and add bits of bacon, ham, onions braized in butter, chopped parsley, a clove of garlic with two cuts, and rice or macaroni. Put in those vegetables first which require most cooking, and do not make the broth too thin. Leave the garlic in for a quarter of an hour only.

No. 41. Minestra of Rice and Cabbage

Ingredients: Rice, cabbage, stock, ham, tomato sauce.

Cut off the stalk and all the hard outside leaves of a cabbage, wash it and cut it up, but not too small, then drain and cook it in good stock and add two ounces of boiled rice. This minestre is improved by adding a little chopped ham and a few spoonsful of tomato sauce.

No. 42. Minestra of Rice and Celery

Ingredients: Celery, rice, stock.

Cut up a head of celery and remove all the green parts, then boil it in good stock and add two ounces of rice, and boil till it is well cooked.

FISH

No. 43. Anguilla alla Milanese (Eels).

Ingredients: Eels, butter, flour, stock, bay leaves, salt, pepper, Chablis, a macedoine of vegetables.

Cut up a big eel and fry it in two ounces of butter, and when it is a good colour add a tablespoonful of flour, about half a pint of stock, a glass of Chablis, a bay leaf, pepper, and salt, and boil till it is well cooked. In the meantime boil separately all sorts of vegetables, such as carrots, cauliflower, celery, beans, tomatoes, &c. Take out the pieces of eel, but keep them hot, whilst you pass the liquor which forms the sauce through a sieve and add the vegetables to this. Let them boil a little longer and arrange them in a dish; place the pieces of eel on them and cover with the sauce. It is most important that the eels should be served very hot.

Any sort of fish will do as well for this dish.

No. 44. Filletti di Pesce alla Villeroy (Fillets of Fish)

Ingredients: Fish, flour, butter, Villeroy.

Any sort of fish will do, turbot, sole, trout, &c. Cut it into fillets, flour them over and cook them in butter in a covered stewpan; then make a Villeroy (No. 18), dip the fillets into it and fry them in clarified butter.

No. 45. Astachi all'Italiana (Lobster)

Ingredients: Lobsters, Velute sauce, Marsala, butter, forcemeat of fish, olives, anchovy butter, button mushrooms, truffles, lemon, crayfish, Italian sauce.

Two boiled lobsters are necessary. Cut all the flesh of one of the lobsters into fillets and put them into a saucepan with half a cup of Velute sauce (No. 2) and half a glass of Marsala, and boil for a few minutes. Put a crouton of fried bread on an oval dish and cover it with a forcemeat of fish, and on this place the whole lobster, cover it with buttered paper, and put it in a moderate oven just long enough to cook the forcemeat. Then make some quenelles of anchovy butter, olives, and button mushrooms, mix them with Italian sauce (No. 6), and garnish the dish with them, and round the crouton arrange the fillets of lobster with a garnish of slices of truffle. Add a dessert-spoonful of crayfish butter and a good squeeze of lemon juice to the sauce, and serve.

No. 46. Baccala alla Giardiniera (Cod)

Ingredients: Cod or hake, carrots, turnips, butter, herbs.

Boil a piece of cod or hake and break it up into flakes, then cut up two carrots and a turnip; boil them gently, and when they are half boiled drain and put them into a stewpan with an ounce of butter, half a teacup of boiling water, salt, and herbs. When they are well cooked add the fish and serve. Fillets of lemon soles may also be cooked this way.

No. 47. Triglie alla Marinara (Mullet)

Ingredients: Mullet, salt, pepper, onions, parsley, oil, water.

Cut a mullet into pieces and put it into a stewpan (with the lid on), with salt, pepper, a cut-up onion, some chopped parsley, half a wineglass of the finest olive oil and half a pint of water, and in this cook the fish gently. Arrange the fillets on a dish, pour a little of the broth over them, and add the onion and parsley. Instead of mullet you can use cod, hake, whiting, lemon sole, &c.

No. 48. Mullet alla Tolosa

Ingredients: Mullet, butter, salt, onions, parsley, almonds, anchovies, button mushrooms, tomatoes.

Cut off the fins and gills of a mullet, put it in a fireproof dish with two ounces of butter and salt. Cut up a small bit of onion, a sprig of parsley, a few blanched almonds, one anchovy, and a few button mushrooms, previously softened in hot water, and put them over the fish and bake for twenty minutes Then add two tablespoonsful of tomato sauce or puree, and when cooked serve. If you like, use sole instead of mullet.

No. 49. Mullet alla Triestina

Ingredients: Mullet (or sole or turbot), butter, salt half a lemon, Chablis.

Put the fish in a fireproof dish with one and a half ounces of butter, salt, a squeeze of lemon juice, and half a glass of Chablis. Put it on a very, slow fire and turn the fish when necessary. When it is cooked serve in the dish.

No. 50. Whiting alla Genovese

Ingredients: Whiting, butter, pepper, salt, bay leaf claret, parsley, onions, garlic capers, vinegar, Espagnole sauce, mushrooms, anchovies.

Put one or two whiting into a stewpan with two ounces of butter, salt, pepper, two bay leaves, and a glass of claret or Burgundy; cook on a hot fire and turn the fish when necessary. Have ready beforehand a remoulade sauce made in the following manner: Put in a saucepan 1 1/2 ounces of butter, half a teaspoonful of chopped parsley, half an onion, a clove of garlic (with one cut), four capers, one anchovy, all chopped up except the garlic. Then add three tablespoonsful of vinegar and reduce the sauce. Add two glasses of Espagnole sauce (No. 1) and a little good stock; boil it all up (take out the garlic and bay leaves) and pass through a sieve, then pour it over the whiting. Boil it all again for a few minutes, and before serving garnish with a few button mushrooms cooked separately. The remoulade sauce will be much better if made some hours beforehand.

No. 51. Merluzzo in Bianco (Cod)

Ingredients: Cod or whiting, salt, onions, parsley, cloves, turnips, marjoram, chervil, milk.

Boil gently in a big cupful of salted water two onions, one turnip, a pinch of chopped parsley, chervil, and marjoram and four cloves. After half an hour pass this through a sieve (but first take out the cloves), and add an equal quantity of milk and a little cream, and in this cook the fish and serve with the sauce over it.

No. 52. Merluzzo in Salamoia (Cod)

Ingredients: Cod, hake, whiting or red mullet, onions, parsley, mint, marjoram, turnips, mushrooms, chervil, cloves, salt, milk, cream, eggs.

Put a salt-spoonful of salt, two onions, a little parsley, marjoram, mint, chervil, a turnip, a mushroom, and the heads of two cloves into a stewpan and simmer in a cupful of milk for half an hour, then let all the ingredients settle at the bottom, and pass the broth through a hair sieve, and add to it an equal quantity of milk or cream, and in it cook your fish on a slow fire. When the fish is quite cooked, pour off the sauce, but leave a little on the fish to keep it warm; reduce the rest in a bain-marie; stir all the time, so that the milk may not curdle. Thicken the sauce with the yolk of an egg, and when about to serve pour it over the fish.

No. 53. Baccala in Istufato (Haddock)

Ingredients: Haddock or lemon sole, carrots, anchovies, lemon, pepper, butter, onions, flour, white wine, stock.

Stuff a haddock (or filleted lemon sole) with some slices of carrot which have been masked with a paste made of pounded anchovies, very little chopped lemon peel, salt and pepper. Then fry an onion with two cuts across it in butter. Take out the onion as soon as it has become a golden colour, flour the fish and put it in the butter, and when it has been well fried on both sides pour a glass of Marsala over it, and when it is all absorbed add a cup of fowl or veal stock and let it simmer for half an hour, then skim and reduce the sauce, pour it over the fish and serve.

No. 54. Naselli con Piselli (Whiting)

Ingredients: Whiting, onions, parsley, peas, tomatoes, butter, Parmesan, Bechamel sauce.

Cut a big whiting into two or three pieces and fry them slightly in butter, add a small bit of onion, a teaspoonful of chopped parsley and fry for a few minutes more. Then add some peas which have been cooked in salted water, three tablespoonsful of Bechamel sauce (No. 3), and three of tomato puree, and cook all together on a moderate fire.

No. 55. Ostriche alla Livornese (Oysters)

Ingredients: Oysters, parsley, shallot, anchovies, fennel pepper, bread crumbs, cream, lemon.

Detach the oysters from their shells and put then into china shells with their own liquor. Have ready a dessert-spoonful of parsley, shallot, anchovy and very little fennel, add a tablespoonful of bread crumbs and a little pepper, and mix the whole with a little cream. Put some of this mixture on each oyster and then bake them in a moderate fire for a quarter of an hour. At the last minute add a squeeze of lemon juice to each oyster and serve on a folded napkin.

No. 56. Ostriche alla Napolitana (Oysters)

Ingredients: Oysters, parsley, celery, thyme, pepper, garlic, oil, lemon.

Prepare the oysters as above, but rub each shell with a little garlic. Put on each oyster a mixture made of chopped parsley, a little thyme, pepper, and bread crumbs. Then pour a few drops of oil on each shell, put them on the gridiron on an open fire, grill for a few minutes, and add a little lemon juice before serving.

No. 57. Ostriche alla Veneziana (Oysters)

Ingredients: Oysters, butter, shallots, truffles, lemon juice, forcemeat of fish.

Take several oysters out of their shells and cook them in butter, a little chopped shallot, and their own liquor, add a little lemon juice and then put in each of the deeper shells a layer of forcemeat made of fish and chopped truffles, then an oyster or two, and over this again another layer of the forcemeat, cover up with the top shell and put them in a fish kettle and steam them. Then remove the top shell and arrange the shells with the oysters on a napkin and serve.

No. 58. Pesci diversi alla Casalinga (Fish)

Ingredients: Any sort of fish, celery, parsley, carrots, garlic, onion, anchovies, almonds, capers, mushrooms, butter, salt, pepper, flour, tomatoes.

Chop up a stick of celery, a sprig of parsley, a carrot, an onion. Pound up an anchovy in brine (well cleaned, boned, and scaled), four shredded almonds, three capers and two mushrooms. Put all this into a saucepan with one ounce of butter, salt and pepper, and fry for a few minutes, then add a few spoonsful of hot water and a tablespoonful of flour and boil gently for ten minutes, put in the fish and cook it until it is done. If you like, you may add a little tomato sauce.

No. 59. Pesce alla Genovese (Sole or Turbot)

Ingredients: Fish (sole, mullet, or turbot), butter, salt, onion, garlic, carrots, celery, parsley, nutmeg, pepper, spice, mushrooms, tomatoes, flour, anchovies.

Fry an onion slightly in one and a half ounces of butter, add a small cut-up carrot, half a stick of celery, a sprig of parsley, and a salt anchovy (scaled), which will dissolve in the butter. Into this put the fish cut up in pieces, a pinch of spice and pepper, and let it simmer for a few minutes, then add two cut-up mushrooms, a tomato mashed up, and a little flour. Mix all together, and cook for twenty minutes.

No. 60. Sogliole in Zimino (Sole)

Ingredients: Sole, onion, beetroot, butter, celery, tomato sauce or white wine.

Cut up a small onion and fry it slightly in one ounce of butter, then add some slices of beetroot (well-washed and drained), and a little celery cut up; to this add fillets of sole or haddock, salt and pepper. Boil on a moderate on the fish kettle. When the beetroot is nearly cooked add two tablespoonsful of tomato puree and boil till all is well cooked. Instead of the tomato you may use half a glass of Chablis.

No. 61. Sogliole al tegame (Sole)

Ingredients: Sole (or mullet), butter, anchovies, parsley, garlic, capers, eggs.

Put an ounce of butter and an anchovy in a saucepan together with a sole or mullet. Fry lightly for a few minutes, then strew a little pepper and chopped parsley over it, put in a clove of garlic with one cut, and cook for half an hour, but turn the fish over when one side is sufficiently done. A few minutes before taking it off the fire add three capers and stir in the yolk of an egg at the last minute. Do not leave the garlic in more than five minutes.

No. 62. Sogliole alla Livornese (Sole)

Ingredients: Sole, butter, garlic, pepper, salt, tomatoes, fennel.

Fillet a sole and put it in a saute-pan with one and a half ounces of butter and a clove of garlic with one cut in it, then sprinkle over it a little chopped fennel, salt and pepper, and let it cook for a few minutes. Turn over the fillets when they are sufficiently cooked on one side, take out the garlic and cover the fish with a puree of tomatoes at the last.

No. 63. Sogliole alla Veneziana (Sole)

Ingredients: Sole, anchovies, butter, bacon, onion, stock, Chablis, salt, nutmeg, parsley, Spanish olives, one bay leaf.

Fillet a sole and interlard each piece with a bit of anchovy. Tie up the fillets and put them in a saute-pan with two ounces of butter, a slice of bacon or ham, and a few small slices of onion. Cover half over with good stock and a glass of Chablis, and add salt, a pinch of nutmeg, a bunch of parsley, and a bay leaf. Cover with buttered paper, and cook on a slow fire for about an hour. Drain the fish, pass the liquor through a sieve, reduce it to the consistency of a thick sauce, and pour it over the fish. Garnish each fillet with a Spanish olive stuffed with anchovy.

No. 64. Sogliole alla Parmigiana (Sole).*

Ingredients: Sole, Parmesan, butter, cream, cayenne.

Fillet a sole and wipe each piece with a clean cloth, then place them in a fireproof dish, and put a small piece of butter on each fillet. Then make a good white sauce, and mix it with two tablespoonsful of grated Parmesan and half a gill of cream. Cover the fish well with the sauce, and bake in a moderate oven for twenty minutes.

*Lemon soles may be used in any of the above-named dishes.

No. 65. Salmone alla Genovese (Salmon)

Ingredients: Salmon, Genoese sauce (No. 5), butter, lemon.

Boil a bit of salmon, drain it, take off the skin, and mask it with a Genoese sauce, to which add a spoonful of the water in which the salmon has been boiled, and at the last add a pat of fresh butter and a squeeze of lemon juice.

No. 66. Salmone alla Perigo (Salmon)

Ingredients: Salmon, forcemeat of fish, truffles, butter, Madeira, croutons of bread, crayfish tails, anchovy butter.

Cut a bit of salmon into well shaped fillets, and marinate them in lemon juice and a bunch of herbs for two hours, wipe them, put a layer of forcemeat of fish over each, and decorate them with slices of truffle. When put them into a well-buttered saute-pan with half a cup of stock and a glass of Madeira or Marsala, cover with buttered paper, and put them into a moderate oven for twenty minutes. Arrange the fillets in a circle on croutons of bread, garnish the centre with crayfish tails and with truffles cut into dice, a quarter of a pint of Velute sauce (No. 2), and half a teaspoonful of anchovy butter. Glaze the fillets and serve.

No. 67. Salmone alla giardiniera (Salmon)

Ingredients: Salmon, forcemeat of fish, vegetables, butter, Bechamel, and Espagnole sauce.

Prepare the fillets as above (No. 66), and put on each a layer of white forcemeat of fish. Cook a macedoine of vegetables separately, and garnish each fillet with some of it, then cook them in a covered stewpan Put a crouton of bread in an entree dish and garnish it with cooked peas, mixed with Bechamel sauce (No. 3), stock, and butter. Around this place the fillets of fish, leaving the centre with the peas uncovered. Pour some rich Espagnole sauce (No. 1) round the fillets and serve.

No. 68. Salmone alla Farnese (Salmon)

Ingredients: Salmon, oil, lemon juice, thyme, salt, pepper, nutmeg, mayonnaise sauce, lobster butter, gelatine, Velute sauce, olives, anchovy butter, white truffles, mushrooms in oil, crayfish.

Boil a piece of salmon, and when cold cut it into fillets and marinate them for two hours in oil, lemon juice, salt, thyme pepper, and nutmeg. Then make a good mayonnaise and add to it some lobster butter mixed with a little dissolved gelatine and Velute sauce (No. 2). Wipe the fillets and arrange them in a circle on a dish, and pour the mayonnaise over them. Then decorate the border of the dish with aspic jelly, and in the centre put some stoned Spanish olives stuffed with anchovy butter, truffles, mushrooms in oil, and crayfish tails.

No. 69. Salmone alla Santa Fiorentina (Salmon)

Ingredients: Salmon, eggs, mayonnaise, parsley, flour.

Marinate a piece of boiled salmon for an hour; take out the bone and cut the fish into fillets, wipe them, roll them in flour and dip them in eggs beaten up or in mayonnaise sauce, and fry them a good colour. Arrange in a circle on the dish, garnish with fried parsley, and serve with Dutch or mayonnaise sauce. Any fillets of fish may be cooked in this manner.

No. 70. Salmone alla Francesca (Salmon)

Ingredients: Salmon, butter, onions, parsley, salt, pepper, nutmeg, stock, Chablis, Espagnole sauce (No.1) mushrooms, anchovy butter, lemon.

Put a firm piece of salmon in a stewpan with one and a half ounces of butter, an onion cut up, a teaspoonful of chopped parsley (blanched), salt, pepper, very little nutmeg, a cup of stock, and a glass of Chablis. Cook for half an hour over a hot fire, turn the salmon occasionally, and if it gets dry, add a cup of Espagnole sauce. Let it boil until sufficiently cooked, and then put it on a dish. Into the sauce put four mushrooms cooked in white sauce, half a teaspoonful of anchovy butter and a little lemon juice. Pour the sauce over the salmon and serve.

No. 71. Fillets of Salmon in Papiliotte

Ingredients: Salmon, oil, lemon juice, salt, pepper, nutmeg, herbs.

Cut a piece of salmon into fillets, marinate them in oil, lemon juice, salt, pepper, nutmeg, and herbs for two hours. Wipe and put them into paper souffle cases with a little oil, butter, and herbs. Cook them on a gridiron, and serve with a sauce piquante made in the following manner: Half a pint of rich Espagnole sauce (No. 1) and a dessert-spoonful of New Century sauce, warmed up in a bain-marie.

BEEF, MUTTON, VEAL, LAMB

No. 72. Manzo alla Certosina (Fillet of Beef)

Ingredients: Fillet of beef or rump steak, bacon, olive oil, salt, nutmeg, anchovies, herbs, stock, garlic.

Put a piece of very tender rump steak or fillet of beef into a stewpan with two slices of fat bacon and three teaspoonsful of the finest olive oil; season with salt and a tiny pinch of nutmeg; let it cook uncovered, and turn the meat over occasionally. When it is nicely browned add an anchovy minced and mixed with chopped herbs, and a small clove of garlic with one cut across it. Then cover the whole with good stock, put the cover on the stewpan, and when it is all sufficiently cooked, skim the grease off the sauce, pass it through a sieve, and pour it over the beef. Leave the garlic in for five minutes only.

No. 73. Stufato alla Florentina (Stewed Beef)

Ingredients: Beef, mutton, or veal, onions, rosemary, Burgundy, tomatoes, stock, potatoes, butter, garlic.

Cut up an onion and three leaves of rosemary, fry them slightly in an ounce of butter, then add meat (beef, mutton, or veal), cut into fair-sized pieces, salt it and fry it a little, then pour half a glass of Burgundy over it, and add two tablespoonsful of tomato conserve, or better still, fresh tomatoes in a puree. Cover up the stewpan and cook gently, stir occasionally, and add some stock if the stew gets too dry. If you like to add potatoes, cut them up, put them in the stewpan an hour before serving, and cook them with the meat. A clove of garlic with one cut may be added for five minutes.

No. 74. Coscia di Manzo al Forno (Rump Steak)

Ingredients: Rump steak, ham, salt, pepper, spice, fat bacon, onion, stock, white wine.

Lard a bit of good rump steak with bits of lean ham, and season it with salt, pepper, and a little spice, slightly brown it in butter for a few minutes, then cover it with three or four slices of fat bacon and put it into a stewpan with an onion chopped up, a cup of good stock, and half a glass of white wine; cook with the cover on the stewpan for about an hour. You may add a clove of garlic for ten minutes.

No. 75. Polpettine alla Salsa Piccante (Beef Olives)

Ingredients: Beef steak, butter, onions, stock, sausage meat.

Cut some thin slices of beef steak, and on each place a little forcemeat of fowl or veal, to which add a little sausage meat: roll up the slices of beef and cook them with butter and onions, and when they are well browned pour some stock over them, and let them absorb it. Serve with a tomato sauce (No. 10), or sauce piquante made with a quarter of a pint of rich Espagnole (No. 1), and a dessert-spoonful of New Century sauce.

No. 76. Stufato alla Milanese (Stewed Beef)

Ingredients: Rump steak, bacon, ham, salt, pepper, cinnamon, cloves, butter, onions, Burgundy.

Beat a piece of rump steak to make it tender and lard it well, cut up some bits of fat bacon and dust them over with salt, pepper, and a tiny pinch of cinnamon, and put them on the steak. Stick three cloves into the steak, then put it into a stewpan, add a little of the fat of the beef chopped up, an ounce of butter, an onion cut up, and some bits of lean ham. Put in sufficient stock to cover the steak, add a glass of Burgundy, and stew gently until it is cooked.

No. 77. Manzo Marinato Arrosto (Marinated Beef)

Ingredients: Beef, salt, larding bacon, Burgundy, vinegar, spices, herbs, flour.

Beat a piece of rump steak, or fillet to make it tender; sprinkle it well with salt and some chopped herbs, and leave it for an hour; then lard it and marinate it as follows: Half a pint of red wine (Australian Harvest Burgundy is best), half a glass of vinegar, a pinch of spice, and a bouquet of herbs; leave it in this for twenty-four hours then take it out, drain it well sprinkle it with flour, and roast it for twenty minutes before a clear fire, braize it till quite tender, then press and glaze it. The thin end of a sirloin is excellent cooked this way. Serve cold.

No. 78. Manzo con sugo di Barbabietole (Fillet of Beef)

Ingredients: Beef, beetroot, salt.

Cut up three raw beetroots put them into an earthen ware pot and cover them with water. Keep them in some warm place, and allow them to ferment for five, six, or eight days according to the season; the froth at the top of the water will indicate the necessary fermentation. The take out the pieces of beetroot, skim off all the froth, and into the fermented liquor put a good piece of tender rump steak or fillet with some salt. Braize for four hours and serve.

No. 79. Manzo in Insalata (Marinated Beef)

Ingredients: Beef, oil, salt, pepper, vinegar, parsley, capers, mushrooms, olives, vegetables.

Cook a fillet of beef (or the thin end of a sirloin), which has been previously marinated for two days in oil, salt, pepper, vinegar, and chopped parsley. When cold press and glaze it, garnish it with capers, mushrooms preserved in vinegar or gherkins, olives, and any kind of vegetables marinated like the beef. Serve cold.

No. 80. Filetto di Bue con Pistacchi (Fillets of Beef with Pistacchios)

Ingredients: Fillet of beef, oil, salt, flour, pistacchio nuts, gravy.

Cut a piece of tender beef into little fillets, and put a them in a stewpan with a tablespoonful of olive oil and salt. After they have cooked for a few minutes, powder them with flour, and strew over each fillet some chopped pistacchio nuts. Add a few spoonsful of very good boiling gravy, and cook for another half-hour.

No. 81. Scalopini di Riso (Beef with Risotto)

Ingredients: Rump steak, butter, rice, truffles, tongue, stock, mushrooms.

Slightly stew a bit of rump steak with bits of tongue and mushrooms; let it get cold, and cut it into scallops. Butter a pie dish, and garnish the bottom of it with cooked tongue and slices of cooked truffle, then over this put a layer of well-cooked and seasoned risotto (No. 190), then a layer of the scallops of beef, and then another layer of risotto. Heat in a bain-marie, and turn out of the pie dish, and serve with a very good sauce poured round it.

No. 82. Tenerumi alla Piemontese (Tendons of Veal)

Ingredients: Tendons of veal, fowl forcemeat, truffles, risotto (No. 190), a cock's comb, tongue.

Tendons of veal are that part of the breast which lies near the ribs, and forms an opaque gristly substance. Partly braize a fine bit of this joint, and press it between two plates till cold. Cut it up into fillets, and on each spread a thin layer of fowl forcemeat, and decorate with slices of truffle. Put the fillets into a stewpan, cover them with very good stock, and boil till the forcemeat and truffles are quite cooked. Prepare a risotto all'Italiana (No. 190), put it on a dish and decorate it with bits of red tongue cut into shapes, and in the centre put a whole cooked truffle and a white cock's comb, both on a silver skewer. Place the tendons of veal round the dish. Add a good Espagnole sauce (No. 1) and serve.

If you like, leave out the risotto and serve the veal with Espagnole sauce mixed with cooked peas and chopped truffle.

No. 83. Bragiuole di Vitello (Veal Cutlets)

Ingredients: Veal, salt, pepper, butter, bacon, carrots, flour, Chablis, water, lemon.

Cut a bit of veal steak into pieces the size of small cutlets, salt and pepper them, and put them in a wide low stewpan. Add two ounces of butter, a cut-up carrot, and some bits of bacon also cut up. When they are browned, add a spoonful of flour, half a glass of Chablis, and half a glass of water, and cook on a slow fire for half an hour, then take out the cutlets, reduce the sauce, and pass it through a sieve. Put it back on the fire and add an ounce of butter and a good squeeze of lemon, and when hot pour it over the cutlets.

No. 84. Costolette alla Manza (Veal Cutlets)

Ingredients: Veal cutlets (fowl or turkey cutlets), forcemeat, truffles, mushrooms, tongue, parsley, pasta marinate (No. 17).

Cut a few horizontal lines along your cutlets, and on each put a little veal or fowl forcemeat, to which add in equal quantities chopped truffles, tongue, mushrooms, and a little parsley. Over this put a thin layer of pasta marinate, and fry the cutlets on a slow fire.

No. 85. Vitello alla Pellegrina (Breast of Veal)

Ingredients: Breast of veal, butter, onions, sugar, stock, red wine, mushrooms, bacon, salt, flour, bay leaf.

Roast a bit of breast of veal, then glaze over two Spanish onions with butter and a little sugar, and when they are a good colour pour a teacup of stock and a glass of Burgundy over them, and add a few mushrooms, a bay leaf, some salt, and a few bits of bacon. When the mushrooms and onions are cooked, skim off the fat and thicken the sauce with a little flour and butter fried together; pour it over the veal and put the onions and mushrooms round the dish.

No. 86. Frittura Piccata al Marsala (Fillet of Veal)

Ingredients: Veal, butter, Marsala, stock, lemon, bacon.

Cut a tender bit of veal steak into small fillets, cut off all the fat and stringy parts, flour them and fry them in butter. When they are slightly browned add a glass of Marsala and a teacup of good stock, and fry on a very hot fire, so that the fillets may remain tender. Take them off the fire, put a little roll of fried bacon on each, add a squeeze of lemon juice, and serve.

No. 87. Polpettine Distese (Veal Olives)

Ingredients: Veal steak, butter, bread, eggs, pistacchio nuts, spice, parsley.

Cut some slices of veal steak very thin as for veal olives, and spread them out in a well-buttered stewpan. On each slice of veal put half a spoonful of the following mixture: Pound some crumb of bread and mix it with a whole egg; add a little salt, some pistacchio nuts, herbs, and parsley chopped up, and a little butter. Roll up each slice of veal, cover with a sheet of buttered paper, put the cover on the stewpan and cook for three-quarters of an hour in two ounces of butter on a slow fire. Thicken the sauce with a dessert-spoonful of flour and butter fried together.

No. 88. Coste di Vitello Imboracciate (Ribs of Veal)

Ingredients: Ribs of veal, butter, eggs, Parmesan, bread crumbs, parsley.

Cut all the sinews from a piece of neck or ribs of veal, cover the meat with plenty of butter and half cook it on a slow fire, then let it get cold. When cold, egg it over and roll it in bread crumbs mixed with a tablespoonful of grated Parmesan; fry in butter and serve with a garnish of fried parsley and a rich sauce. A dessert-spoonful of New Century sauce mixed with quarter of a pint of good thick stock makes a good sauce. (See No. 226.)

No. 89. Costolette di Montone alla Nizzarda (Mutton Cutlets)

Ingredients: Mutton cutlets, butter, olives, mushrooms, cucumbers.

Trim as many cutlets as you require, and marinate them in vinegar, herbs, and spice for two hours. Before cooking wipe them well and then saute them in clarified butter, and when they are well coloured on both sides and resist the pressure of the finger, drain off the butter and pour four tablespoonsful of Espagnole sauce (No. 1) with a teaspoonful of vinegar and six bruised pepper corns over them. Arrange them on a dish, putting between each cutlet a crouton of fried bread, and garnish with olives stuffed with chopped mushrooms and with slices of fried cucumber.

No. 90. Petto di Castrato all'Italiana (Breast of Mutton)

Ingredients: Breast of mutton, veal, forcemeat, eggs, herbs, spice, Parmesan.

Stuff a breast of mutton with veal forcemeat mixed with two eggs beaten up, herbs, a little spice, and a tablespoonful of grated Parmesan, braize it in stock with a bunch of herbs and two onions. Serve with Italian sauce (No. 6).

No. 91. Petto di Castrato alla Salsa piccante (Breast of Mutton)

Ingredients: Same as No. 90.

When the breast of mutton has been stuffed and cooked as above, let it get cold and then cut it into fillets, flour them over, fry in butter, and serve with tomato sauce piquante (No. 10), or one dessert-spoonful of New Century sauce in a quarter pint of good stock or gravy.

No. 92. Tenerumi d'Agnello alla Villeroy (Tendons of Lamb)

Ingredients: Tendons of lamb, eggs, bread crumbs, truffles, butter, stock, Villeroy sauce.

Slightly cook the tendons (the part of the breast near the ribs) of lamb, press them between two dishes till cold, then cut into a good shape and dip them into a Villeroy sauce (No. 18) egg and bread-crumb, and saute them in butter. When about to serve, put them in a dish with very good clear gravy. A teaspoonful of chopped mint and a tablespoonful of chopped truffles mixed with the bread crumbs will be a great improvement.

No. 93. Tenerumi d' Agnello alla Veneziana (Tendons of Lamb)

Ingredients: Tendons of lamb, butter, parsley, onions, stock.

Fry the tendons of lamb in butter together with a teaspoonful of chopped parsley and an onion. Serve with good gravy.

No. 94. Costolette d' Agnello alla Costanza (Lamb Cutlets)

Ingredients: Lamb cutlets, butter, stock, cocks' combs, fowl's liver, mushrooms.

Fry as many lamb cutlets as you require very sharply in butter, drain off the butter and replace it with some very good stock or gravy. Make a ragout of cocks' combs, bits of fowl's liver and mushrooms all cut up; add a white sauce with half a gill of cream mixed with it, and with this mask the cutlets, and saute them for fifteen minutes.

TONGUE, SWEETBREAD, CALF'S HEAD, LIVER, SUCKLING PIG

No. 95. Timballo alla Romana

Ingredients: Cold fowl, game, or sweetbread, butter, lard, flour, Parmesan, truffles, macaroni, onions, cream.

Make a light paste of two ounces of butter, two of lard, and half a pound of flour, and put it in the larder for two hours. In the meantime boil a little macaroni and let it get cold, then line a plain mould with the paste, and fill it with bits of cut-up fowl, or game, or sweetbread, bits of truffle cut in small dice, grated Parmesan, and a little chopped onion. Put these ingredients in alternately, and after each layer add enough cream to moisten. Fill the mould quite full, then roll out a thin paste for the top and press it well together at the edges to keep the cream from boiling out. Bake it in a moderate oven for an hour and a half, turn it out of the mould, and serve with a rich brown sauce. Decorate the top with bits of red tongue and truffles cut into shapes or with a little chopped pistacchio nut.

No. 96. Timballo alla Lombarda

Ingredients: Macaroni, fowl or game, eggs, stock, Velute sauce (No. 2), tongue, butter, truffles.

Butter a smooth mould, then boil some macaroni, but take care that it is in long pieces. When cold, take the longest bits and line the bottom of the mould, making the macaroni go in circles; and when you come to the end of one piece, join on the next as closely as possible until the whole mould is lined; paint it over now and then with white of egg beaten up; then mask the whole inside with a thin layer of forcemeat of fowl, which should also be put on with white of egg to make it adhere; then cut up the bits of macaroni which remain, warm them up in some good fowl stock and Velute sauce much reduced, a little melted butter, some bits of truffle cut into dice, tongue, fowl, or game also cut up in pieces. When the mould is full, put on another layer of forcemeat, steam for an hour, then turn out and serve with a very good brown sauce.

No. 97. Lingua alla Visconti (Tongue)

Ingredients: Tongue, glaze, bread, spinach, white grapes, port.

Soak a smoked tongue in fresh water for forty-eight hours, then boil it till it is tender. Peel off the skin, cut the tongue in rather thick slices, and glaze them. Prepare an oval border of fried bread, cover it with spinach about two inches thick, and on this arrange the slices of tongue. Fill in the centre of the dish with white grapes cooked in port or muscat.

No. 98. Lingua di Manzo al Citriuoli (Tongue with Cucumber)

Ingredients: Ox tongue, salt, pepper, nutmeg, parsley, bacon, veal, carrots, onions, thyme, bay leaves, cloves, stock.

Gently boil an ox tongue until you can peel off the skin, then lard it, season it with salt, pepper, nutmeg, and chopped parsley, and boil it with some bits of bacon, ham, veal, a carrot, an onion, two bay leaves, thyme and two cloves. Pour some good stock over it and let it simmer gently until it is cooked. Put the tongue on a dish and garnish it with slices of fried cucumber. Boil the cucumber for five minutes before you fry it, to take away the bitter taste. Serve the tongue with a sauce piquante, made with one dessert-spoonful of New Century sauce to a quarter pint of good Espangole sauce (No. 1).

No. 99. Lingue di Castrato alla Cuciniera (Sheep's Tongues)

Ingredients: Sheep's tongues, bacon, beef, onions, herbs, spice, eggs, butter, flour.

Cook three or four sheep's tongues in good stock, and add some slices of bacon, bits of beef, two onions, a bunch of herbs, and a pinch of spice. Let them get cold, flour them and mask them with egg beaten up and fry quickly in butter. Serve with Italian sauce (No. 6)

No. 100. Lingue di Vitello all'Italiana (Calves' Tongues)

Ingredients: Calves' tongues, salt, butter, stock, water, glaze, potatoes, ham, truffles, sauce piquante.

Rub a good handful of salt into two or three calves' tongues and leave them for twenty-four hours, then wash off all the salt and soak them in fresh water for two hours. Stew them gently till tender, take them out, skin and braize them in butter and good stock for half an hour. Let them get cold and cut them into slices about half an inch thick; put the slices into a buttered saute-pan and cover them with a good thick glaze; let them get quite hot and then arrange them on a border of potatoes, and garnish each slice with round shapes of cooked ham and truffle. Fill the centre with any vegetables you like; fried cucumber is excellent, but if you use it do not forget to boil it for five minutes before you fry it to take away the bitter taste. Serve with a sauce piquante (No. 10, or No. 226).

No. 101. Porcelletto alla Corradino (Suckling Pig)

Ingredients: Suckling pig, ham, eggs, Parmesan, truffles, mushrooms, garlic, bay leaves, coriander seeds, pistacchio nuts, veal forcemeat, suet, bacon, herbs, spice.

Bone a Suckling pig, remove all the inside and fill it with a stuffing made of veal forcemeat mixed with a little chopped suet, ham, bacon, herbs, two tablespoonsful of finely chopped pistacchio nuts, a pinch of spice, six coriander seeds, two tablespoonsful of grated Parmesan, cuttings of truffles and mushrooms all bound together with eggs. Sew the pig up and braize it in a big stewpan with bits of bacon, a clove of garlic with two cuts, a bunch of herbs and one bay leaf, for half an hour. Then pour off the gravy, cover the pig with well-buttered paper, and finish cooking it in the oven. Garnish the top with vegetables and truffles cut into shapes, slices of lemon and sprigs of parsley. Serve with a good sauce piquante (No. 229). Do not leave the garlic in for more than ten minutes.

No. 102. Porcelletto da Latte in Galantina (Suckling Pig)

Ingredients: Suckling pig, forcemeat of fowl, bacon, truffles, pistacchio nuts, ham, lemon, veal, bay leaves, salt, carrots, onions, shallots, parsley, stock, Chablis, gravy.

Bone a Suckling pig all except its feet, but be careful not to cut the skin on its back. Lay it out on a napkin and line it inside with a forcemeat of fowl and veal about an inch thick, over this put a layer of bits of marinated bacon, slices of truffle, pistacchio nuts, cooked ham, and some of the flesh of the pig, then another layer of forcemeat until the pig's skin is fairly filled. Keep its shape by sewing it lightly together, then rub it all over with lemon juice and cover it with slices of fat bacon, roll it up and stitch it in a pudding cloth. Then put the bones and cuttings into a stewpan with bits of bacon and veal steak cut up, two bay leaves, salt, a carrot, an onion, a shallot, and a bunch of parsley. Into this put the pig with a bottle of white wine and sufficient stock to cover it, and cook on a slow fire for three hours. Then take it out, and when cold take off the pudding-cloth. Pass the liquor through a hair sieve, and, if necessary, add some stock; reduce and clarify it. Decorate the dish with this jelly and serve cold.

No. 103. Ateletti alla Sarda

Ingredients: Veal or fowl, ox palates, stock, tongue, truffles, butter, mushrooms, sweetbread.

Soak two ox palates in salted water for four hours, then boil them until the rough skin comes off, and cook them in good stock for six hours, press them between two plates and let them get cold. Roll some forcemeat of veal or fowl in flour, cut it into small pieces about the size of a cork, boil them in salted water, let them get cold and cut them into circular pieces. Cut the ox palates also into circular pieces the same size as the bits of forcemeat, then thinner circles of cooked tongue and truffles. String these pieces alternately on small silver skewers. Reduce to half its quantity a pint of Velute sauce (No. 2), and add the cuttings of the truffles, mushroom trimmings, bits of sweetbread, and a squeeze of lemon juice. Let it get cold and then mask the atelets (or skewers with the forcemeat, &c.) with it, and fry them quickly in butter. Fry a large oval crouton of bread, scoop out the centre and fill it with fried slices of cucumber and truffles boiled in a little Chablis. Stick the skewers into the crouton and pour the sauce round it.

For a maigre dish use fillets of fish, truffles, mushrooms, and Bechamel sauce (No. 3). The cucumber should be boiled for five minutes before it is fried.

No. 104. Ateletti alla Genovese

Ingredients: Veal, sweetbread, calf's brains, ox palates, mushrooms, fonds d'artichauds, cocks' combs, eggs, Parmesan, bread crumbs.

Cook two ox palates as in the last recipe, then take equal quantities of veal steak, sweetbread, calf's brains, equal quantities of mushrooms, fonds d'artichauds, and cocks' combs. Fry them all in butter except the palates, but be careful to put the veal in first, as it requires longer cooking; the brains should go in last. Then put all these ingredients on a cutting board and add the palates (cooked separately); cut them all into pieces of equal size, either round or square, but keep the ingredients separate, and string them alternately on silver skewers, as in the last recipe. Then pound up all the cuttings and add a little crumb of bread soaked in stock, the yolks of three eggs, the whites of two well beaten up, two dessert-spoonsful of grated Parmesan, salt to taste, and chopped truffles. Mix all this well together and mask the atelets with it; egg and bread crumb them and fry in butter. When they are a good colour, serve with fried parsley.

No. 105. Testa di Vitello alla Sorrentina (Calf's Head)

Ingredients: Calf's head, veal, sweetbread, truffles, mushrooms, pistacchio nuts, eggs, herbs, spice, stock, bacon, ham.

Boil a half calf's head well, and when it is half cold, bone it and fill it with a stuffing of veal, the calf's brains, sweetbread, truffles, mushrooms, pistacchio nuts, the yolks of two eggs, herbs, and a little spice. Then stitch it up and braize it in good stock, with some slices of bacon, ham, and a bunch of herbs. Serve with brain sauce mixed with cream.

No. 106. Testa di Vitello con Salsa Napoletana (Calf's Head)

Ingredients: Calf's head, calf's liver, bacon, suet, truffles, almonds, olives, calf's brains, capers, spice, coriander seeds, herbs, ham, stock.

Boil half a calf's head, bone it and fill it with a stuffing made of four ounces of calf's liver, well chopped up and pounded in a mortar; two ounces of bacon, one ounce of suet, three truffles, six almonds, three olives, six coriander seeds, six capers, the calf's brains, a pinch of spice and a teaspoonful of chopped herbs. Roll up the head, tie it up and put it into a stewpan with some bits of bacon, ham, and very good stock, and stew it slowly. Serve with Neapolitan sauce (No.12), or with tomato sauce piquante (No. 10).

No. 107. Testa di Vitello alla Pompadour (Calf's Head)

Ingredients: Calf's head, calf's brains, cream, eggs, truffles, cinnamon, stock, butter, Parmesan.

Boil and bone half a calf's head and fill it with a stuffing made of the calf's brains, a gill of cream, the yolks of two eggs, two truffles cut up, a little chopped ham, and a tiny pinch of cinnamon. Boil it in good stock, and when it is sufficiently cooked take it out and mask it all over with a mixture of butter, yolk of egg, and a tablespoonful of grated Parmesan, then brown it in the oven and serve hot.

No. 108. Testa di Vitello alla Sanseverino (Calf's Head)

Ingredients: Calf's head, sweetbread, fowl's liver, anchovies, herbs, capers, garlic, bacon, ham, Malmsey or Muscat.

Boil and bone half a calf's head, and fill it with a stuffing made of half a pound of sweetbread, a fowl's liver, two anchovies, a teaspoonful of chopped herbs, a few chopped capers, and the calf's brains. Roll the head up, stitch it together and braize it in half a tumbler of Malmsey or Australian Muscat (Burgoyne's), half a cup of very good white stock, some bits of ham and bacon, and a clove of garlic with two cuts. Cook it gently for four hours and serve it with its own sauce. Do not leave the garlic in longer than ten minutes.

No. 109. Testa di Vitello in Frittata (Calf's Head)

Ingredients: Calf's head, eggs, Parmesan, ham, pepper, butter, croutons.

A good rechauffe' of calf's head may be made in the following manner: After the head has been well boiled in good stock, cut it into slices and mask these with a mixture of eggs well beaten up, grated Parmesan, pepper, and chopped ham. Fry in butter, and garnish with fried parsley and fried croutons. Serve with a sauce made of a quarter of a pint of good Bechamel (No. 3) and a dessert-spoonful of New Century sauce.

No. 110. Zampetti (Calves' Feet)

Ingredients: Calves' or pigs' feet, butter, leeks or small onions, parsley, salt, pepper, stock, tomatoes, eggs, cheese, cinnamon.

Blanch and bone two or more calves' or pigs' feet and put them into a stewpan with butter, leeks, or onions, chopped parsley, salt, pepper, and a little stock. Let them boil till the liquid is somewhat reduced, then add good meat gravy and two tablespoonsful of tomato puree, and just before taking the stewpan off the fire, add the yolks of two eggs beaten up, a tablespoonful of grated cheese, and a tiny pinch of cinnamon. Mix all well together and serve very hot.

No. 111. Bodini Marinati

Ingredients: Veal forcemeat, truffles, sweetbread, mushrooms, herbs, flour, pasta marinate (No. 17), tongue, butter.

Make a mixture of truffles, tongue, sweetbread, mushrooms, and herbs, all chopped up, and add it to a forcemeat of veal, the proportions being two-thirds veal forcemeat and the other ingredients one third. Mix this well and form it into little balls about the size of a pigeon's egg, flour them and mask them all over with pasta marinate (No. 17). Fry them in butter over a slow fire, so that the balls may be well cooked through, and when they are the right colour dry them in a napkin and serve very hot.

These bodini may be made with various ingredients; they will be most delicate with a forcemeat of fowl and bits of brain mixed with herbs, truffle, cooked ham, or tongue. They are also excellent made with fish (sole, mullet, turbot, &c.), either cooked or raw, and marinated in lemon, salt, pepper, oil, nutmeg, and parsley.

No. 112. Animelle alla Parmegiana (Sweetbread)

Ingredients: Sweetbread, bread crumbs, Parmesan, butter.

Blanch as many sweetbreads as you require, and then roll them in bread crumbs mixed with grated Parmesan, salt, and pepper; wrap them up in buttered grease-proof paper and grill them. When they are cooked, take off the paper, and serve with a good sauce in a sauce-boat.

No. 113. Animelle in Cartoccio (Sweetbread)

Ingredients: Sweetbread, butter, herbs, salt, pepper, bread crumbs, Parmesan, lemons, gravy, tomatoes.

Blanch a pound of sweetbread cuttings, mix it with two ounces of melted butter, chopped herbs, salt, and pepper, and put it into paper souffle cases. Then strew over each some bread crumbs mixed with grated Parmesan, put the cases in the oven, and when they are browned serve either with good gravy and lemon juice or with tomato sauce (No. 9).

No. 114. Animelle all'Italiana (Sweetbread)

Ingredients: Sweetbread, butter, onions, salt, herbs, eggs, glaze, Risotto (No. 190), truffles, quenelles of fowl, Espagnole sauce, white sauce.

Blanch as many sweetbreads as you require, cut them into quarters and saute them in butter with a small onion cut up, salt, and a bunch of herbs. Then pour over them two cups of white sauce and cook gently for twenty minutes; take out the sweetbreads and put them in a stewpan. Reduce the sauce, and add to it a mixture made of the yolks of four eggs, one and a half ounce of butter and a teaspoonful of glaze; pass it through a sieve, pour it over the sweetbreads, and keep them warm in a bain-marie. Have ready a good Risotto all'Italiana (No. 190), and put it into a border mould (but first decorate the inside of the mould with slices of truffle), put it in a moderate oven, and when it is warm turn it out on a dish. Place the sweetbreads on the risotto and fill in the centre with quenelles of fowl and Espagnole sauce (No. 1).

No. 115. Animelle Lardellate (Sweetbread)

Ingredients: Sweetbreads, larding, bacon, stock, a macedoine of vegetables.

Blanch two sweetbreads, lard them, and cook them very slowly in good stock. Skim the stock and reduce it to a glaze to cover the sweetbreads. Then cut them into three or four pieces and arrange them round a dish, but see that the larding is well glazed over. In the centre of the dish place a piece of bread in the shape of a cup and fill this with a macedoine of vegetables.

No. 116. Frittura di Bottoni e di Animelle (Sweetbread and Mushrooms)

Ingredients: Sweetbread, fresh button mushrooms, flour, bread crumbs, salt, pepper, parsley, butter, lemons.

Peel some button mushrooms and cut them in halves. Boil a sweetbread, and cut it into pieces about the same size as the mushrooms, flour, egg, and bread crumb them, and fry in butter; then serve with a garnish of fried parsley. Hand cut lemons with this dish.

No. 117. Cervello in Fili serbe (Calf's Brains)

Ingredients: Calf's brains, stock, butter, parsley, lemon.

Boil half a calf's brain in good stock for ten minutes then drain and pour a little melted butter and the juice of half a lemon over the brain; add some chopped parsley fried for one minute in butter, and serve as hot as possible.

No. 118. Cervello alla Milanese (Calf's Brains)

Ingredients: Calf's brains, eggs, bread crumbs, butter.

Scald a calf's brain and let it get cold. Wipe it on a cloth, and get it as dry as possible, then cut it into pieces about the size of a walnut, egg and bread crumb them, fry in butter, and strew a little salt over them.

No. 119. Cervello alla Villeroy (Calf's Brains)

Ingredients: Calf's brains, eggs, flour, mushrooms, Velute sauce.

Scald a calf's brain, and when cold cut it up and mask each piece with a thick sauce made of well-reduced Velute (No. 2), mixed with chopped cooked mushrooms; flour them over and dip them into the yolk of an egg, and fry as quickly as possible.

No. 120. Frittura of Liver and Brains

Ingredients: Calf's liver and brains (or lamb's or pig's fry), butter, ham, flour, puff pastry.

Cut up half a pound of liver in small slices, flour and fry them in butter or dripping, together with a calf's or pig's or sheep's brain, previously scalded and also cut up. Serve with bits of fried ham and little diamond-shaped pieces of puff pastry.

No. 121. Cervello in Frittata Montano (Calf's Brains)

Ingredients: Calf's brains, stock, cream, eggs, spice, Parmesan, butter.

Boil a calf's brain in good stock for ten minutes, let it get cold, cut it up into little balls, and mask each piece with a mixture made of half a gill of cream, the yolks of two eggs, a little spice, a tablespoonful of grated Parmesan, and the whites of two eggs well beaten up. Fry the balls in butter, and serve as hot as possible. You may mask and cook the calf's brain without cutting it up, if you prefer it so.

No. 122. Marinata di Cervello alla Villeroy (Calf's Brains)

Ingredients: Calf's brains, stock, Bechamel sauce, eggs, butter, lemon, forcemeat of fowl, flour.

Boil a calf's or sheep's brain in good stock, wipe it well, and cut it up. Reduce a pint of Bechamel (No. 3), and add to it the yolks of three eggs, an ounce of butter, and the juice of a lemon. When it boils throw in the cut-up brain; let it cool, then take out the brain and form it into little balls about the size of a small walnut. Make a forcemeat of fowl, and add a dessert-spoonful of flour to it, and spread it out very thin on a paste-board, and into this wrap the balls of brain, each separately. Dip them into a pasta marinate (No. 17), and fry them a golden brown.

No. 123. Minuta alla Milanese (Lamb's Sweetbread)

Ingredients: Lamb's sweetbread, butter, onions, stock, Chablis, salt, lemon, herbs, cocks' combs, fowls' livers.

Cut up equal quantities of lamb's sweetbreads, cocks' combs, fowls' livers in pieces about the size of a filbert, flour and fry them slightly in butter and a small bit of onion, add half a glass of Chablis, a cup of good stock, and a bunch of herbs. Reduce the sauce, and thicken it with a tablespoonful of butter and flour fried together. Make a border of Risotto all'Italiana (No. 190), and put the sweetbread, &c., together with the sauce in the centre.

No. 124. Animelle al Sapor di Targone (Lamb's Fry)

Ingredients: Lamb's fry, ham, garlic, larding bacon, spice, herbs, butter, flour, stock.

The lamb's fry should be nearly all sweetbread, and very little liver. Lard each piece with bacon and ham, and roll it in chopped herbs and a pinch of pounded spice. Then dip it in flour and braize in good stock, to which add three ounces of butter, some bits of bacon, ham, a bay leaf, herbs, and a clove of garlic with two cuts. Cook until the fry is well glazed over, and serve with Tarragon sauce (No. 8). Do not leave the garlic in longer than ten minutes.

No. 125. Fritto Misto alla Villeroy

Ingredients: Cocks' combs, calf's brains, sweetbread, stock, truffles, mushrooms, Villeroy, eggs, bread crumbs.

Cook some big cocks' combs, bits of calf s brains, and sweetbread in good stock, then drain them and marinate them slightly in lemon juice and herbs. Prepare a Villeroy (No. 18), and add to it cuttings of sweetbread, brains, truffles, mushrooms, &c. When it is cold, mask the cocks' combs and other ingredients with it, egg and bread-crumb them, and fry them a golden brown.

No. 126. Fritto Misto alla Piemontese

Ingredients: Sweetbread, calf s brains, ox palate, flour, eggs, Chablis, salt, herbs butter.

Make a thin paste with a tablespoonful of flour, the yolks of two eggs, two Spoonsful of Chablis, and a little salt. Mix this up well, and if it is too thick add a little water. Beat up the whites of the two eggs into a snow. In the meantime blanch a sweetbread, half a calf's brain, and a few bits of cooked ox palate; boil them all up with a bunch of herbs; cut them into pieces about the size of a walnut, and dip them into the paste so that each piece is well covered, then dip them into the beaten-up whites of egg, and fry them very quickly in butter. This fry is generally served with a garnish of French beans, which should not be cut up, but half boiled, then dried, floured over and fried together with the other ingredients. The ox palates should be boiled for at least six hours before you use them in this dish.

No. 127. Minuta di Fegatini (Ragout of Fowls' Livers)

Ingredients: Fowls' or turkeys' livers, flour, butter, parsley, onions, salt, pepper, stock, Chablis.

Cut the livers in half, flour them, and fry lightly in butter with chopped parsley, very little chopped onion, salt and pepper, then add a quarter pint of boiling stock and half a glass of Chablis, and cook until the sauce is somewhat reduced. You can also cook the livers simply in good meat gravy, but in this case they should not be floured. Serve with a border of macaroni (No. 183), or Risotto (No. 190), or Polenta (No. 187).

No. 128. Minuta alla Visconti (Chickens' Livers)

Ingredients: Fowls' livers, eggs, cheese, butter, cream, cayenne pepper.

Braize two fowls' livers in butter, then pound them up, and mix with a little cream, a tablespoonful of grated cheese and a dust of cayenne.

Spread this rather thickly over small squares of toast, and keep them hot whilst you make a custard with half an ounce of butter, an egg well beaten up, and a tablespoonful of cheese. Stir it over the fire till thick and then spread it on the hot toast. Serve very hot. This makes a good savoury.

No. 129. Croutons alla Principesca

Ingredients: Croutons, tongue, sweetbread, truffles, fowl or game, Velute sauce, stock, eggs, butter.

Fry a bit of bread in butter till it is a light brown colour, then cut it into heart-shaped pieces. Prepare a ragout with bits of tongue, sweetbread, fowl or game, truffles, two or three spoonsful of well-reduced Velute sauce (No. 2), and two or three of reduced gravy. Put a spoonful of the ragout in each crouton, and over it a layer of fowl forcemeat half an inch thick; trim the edges neatly, glaze them with the yolk of eggs beaten up, and put them in a buttered fireproof dish in the oven for twenty minutes. Then glaze them with reduced stock and serve hot.

For a maigre dish use fish for the ragout and forcemeat.

No. 130. Croutons alla Romana

Ingredients: Bread, fowl forcemeat, tongue, truffles, herbs, cream, stock, butter, flour, eggs.

Cut a bit of crumb of bread into round or square shapes, and on each put a spoonful of fowl or rabbit forcemeat, a little chopped tongue, and a slight flavouring of chopped herbs; cover with a slice of bread the same shape as the underneath piece, put them in a buttered fireproof dish, and moisten them well with cream, butter, and stock. Cook until all the liquor is absorbed, but turn them over so that both sides may be well cooked, then flour and dip them into beaten-up eggs; fry them a good colour and serve very hot.

For a maigre dish use forcemeat of fish or lobster, and more cream instead of stock.

FOWL, DUCK, GAME, HARE, RABBIT

No. 131. Soffiato di Cappone (Fowl Souffle)

Ingredients: Fowl, Bechamel, stock, semolina flour, potatoes, salt, eggs, butter, smoked tongue or ham.

Prepare a puree of fowl or turkey and a small quantity of grated tongue or ham, and whilst you are pounding the meat add some good gravy or stock. Then make a Bechamel sauce (No. 3) and add two table-spoonsful of semolina flour, a boiled potato and salt to taste, boil it up and add the puree of fowl, then let it get nearly cold, add yolks of eggs and the white beaten up into a snow. (For one pint of the puree use the yolks of three eggs.) Pour the whole into a buttered souffle case, and half an hour before serving put it in a moderate oven and serve hot. You can use game instead of fowl, and serve in little souffle cases.

No. 132. Pollo alla Fiorentina (Chicken)

Ingredients: Fowl, butter, vegetables, rice or macaroni, peppercorns, stock, ham, tomatoes, bay leaves, onions, cloves, Liebig.

Roll up a fowl in buttered paper and put it in the oven in a fireproof dish with all kinds of vegetables and a few peppercorns. Leave it there for about two hours, then put the fowl and vegetables into two quarts of good stock and let it simmer for one hour; serve on well-boiled rice or macaroni and pour the following sauce over it. Sauce: Two pounds tomatoes, one big cup of good stock, a quarter pound of chopped ham, three bay leaves, one onion stuck with cloves, one teaspoonful of Liebig. Simmer an hour and a half.

No. 133. Pollo all'Oliva (Chicken)

Ingredients: Fowl, onions, celery, salt, parsley, carrots, butter, stock, olives, tomatoes.

Cut up half an onion, a stick of celery, a sprig of parsley, a carrot, and cook them all in a quarter pound of butter. Into this put a fowl cut up and let it act brown all over, turn when necessary and then baste it with boiling stock. Add four Spanish olives cut up and four others pounded in a mortar, eight whole olives and three tablespoonsful of tomato puree reduced, and when the fowl is well cooked pour the sauce over it.

No. 134. Pollo alla Villereccia (Chicken)

Ingredients: Fowl, butter, flour, stock, bacon, ham, mushrooms, onions, cloves, eggs, cream, lemons.

Cut up a fowl into quarters and put it into a saucepan with three ounces of butter and a tablespoonful of flour Put it on the fire, and when it is well browned add half a pint of stock, bits of bacon and ham, butter, three mushrooms (previously boiled), an onion stuck with three cloves. When this is cooked skim off the grease, pass the sauce through a sieve, and add the yolks of two eggs mixed with two tablespoonsful of cream. Lastly, add a squeeze of lemon juice to the sauce and pour it over the fowl.

No. 135. Pollo alla Cacciatora (Chicken)

Ingredients: The same as No. 134 and tomatoes.

Cook the fowl exactly as above, but add either a puree of tomatoes or tomato sauce.

No. 136. Pollastro alla Lorenese (Fowl)

Ingredients: Fowl, butter, parsley, lemon, small onions, bread crumbs.

Cut up a fowl and put it into a frying pan with two ounces of butter, one onion cut up and a sprig of chopped parsley, salt and pepper; put it on the fire and cook it, but turn the pieces several times: then take them out and roll them whilst hot in bread crumbs, and fry them. Serve with cut lemons.

No. 137. Pollastro in Fricassea al Burro (Fowl)

Ingredients: Fowl, butter, fat bacon, ham, mushrooms, truffles, herbs, spice, gravy.

Cut up a fowl and cook it in a fricassee of butter, bacon, ham, herbs, mushrooms, truffles, spice, and good gravy or stock. Serve in its own gravy.

No. 138. Pollastro in istufa di Pomidoro (Braized Fowl)

Ingredients: Fowl, bacon, ham, bay leaf, spice, garlic, Burgundy, tomatoes.

Braize a fowl with bits of fat bacon, ham, a bay leaf, a clove of garlic with one cut in it, a pinch of spice, and a glass of Burgundy. Only leave the garlic in for five minutes. When cooked serve with tomato sauce (No. 9).

No. 139. Cappone con Riso (Capon with Rice)

Ingredients: Capon, veal forcemeat, fat bacon, stock, rice, truffles, mushrooms, cocks' combs, kidneys or fowls' liver, supreme sauce, milk, Chablis.

Stuff a fine capon with a good firm forcemeat made of veal, tongue, ham, and chopped truffles; cover it with larding bacon; tie it up in buttered paper, and cook it in very good white stock. In the meantime boil four ounces of rice in milk till quite stiff, mix in some chopped truffles, and make ten little timbales of it. Take out the capon when it is sufficiently cooked and place it on a dish; garnish it with cooked mushrooms, cocks' combs, kidneys, or fowls' livers, and pour a sauce supreme (No. 16) over it; round the dish place the timbales of rice, and between each put a whole truffle cooked in white wine. Serve a sauce supreme in a sauce bowl.

No. 140. Dindo Arrosto alla Milanese (Roast Turkey)

Ingredients: Turkey, sausage meat, prunes, chestnuts, a pear, butter, Marsala, salt, rosemary, bacon, carrot, onion, turnip, garlic.

Blanch for seven or eight minutes three prunes, quarter of a pound of sausage meat, three tablespoonsful of chestnut puree, two small slices of bacon, half a cooked pear, and saute them in butter; chop up the liver and gizzard of the turkey, mix them with the other ingredients, and add half a glass of Marsala; use this as a stuffing for the turkey, and first braize it for three quarters of an hour with salt, butter, a blade of rosemary, bits of fat bacon, a carrot, a turnip, an onion, three cloves, and a clove of garlic with a cut; then roast it before a clear fire for about twenty minutes; put it back into the sauce till it is ready to serve. Only leave the garlic in ten minutes.

No. 141. Tacchinotto all'Istrione (Turkey Poult)

Ingredients: A turkey poult, ham, mace, bay leaves, lemons, water, salt, onions, parsley, celery, carrots, Chablis.

Truss a turkey poult, and cover it all over with slices of ham or bacon, put two bay leaves and four slices of lemon on it, and sprinkle with a small pinch of mace, then sew it up tight in a dishcloth, and stew it in good stock, salt, an onion, parsley, a stick of celery, a carrot, and a pint of Chablis; cook for an hour, take it out of the cloth, and pour a good rich sauce over it. It is also good cold with aspic jelly.

No. 142. Fagiano alla Napoletana (Pheasant)

Ingredients: Pheasant, macaroni, gravy, butter, Parmesan, tomatoes.

Lard a pheasant, roast it, and serve it on a layer of macaroni cooked with good reduced gravy, two ounces of butter, a tablespoonful of grated Parmesan, and a puree of tomatoes. Serve with Neapolitan sauce (No. 12) in a sauce bowl.

No. 143. Fagiano alla Perigo (Pheasant)

Ingredients: Pheasant, butter, truffles, larding bacon, Madeira.

Make a mixture of three tablespoonsful of chopped truffles, three ounces of butter and a little salt, and with this stuff a pheasant. Then cover it with slices of fat bacon and keep it in a cool place till next day. A few hours before serving, roast the pheasant and baste it well with melted butter and a wine-glass of Madeira or Marsala. Make a crouton of fried bread the shape of your dish, and over this put a Layer of forcemeat of fowl and a number of small fowl quenelles; cover them with buttered paper, then put the dish in the oven for a few minutes so as to settle the forcemeat. When the pheasant is cooked, place it on the crouton and garnish it with slices of truffle which have been previously cooked in Madeira, and serve with a Perigord sauce.

No. 144. Anitra Selvatica (Wild Duck)

Ingredients: Wild duck, butter, fowls' livers, Marsala, gravy, turnips, carrots, parsley, mushrooms.

Cut a wild duck into quarters and put it into a stewpan with two fowls' livers cut up and fried in butter. When the pieces of duck are coloured on both sides, pour off the butter, and in its place pour a glass of Marsala, a cup of stock, and a cup of Espagnole sauce (No.1), and cook gently for ten minutes. In the meantime shape and blanch six young turnips and as many young carrots, put them into a stewpan, and on the top of them put the pieces of wild duck, liver, &c. Pass the liquor through a sieve and pour it over the wild duck, add a bunch of parsley and other herbs and five little mushrooms cut up, and cook on a slow fire for half an hour. Skim the sauce, pass it through a sieve and add a pinch of sugar. Put the pieces of wild duck in an entree dish, add the vegetables, &c., pour the sauce over and serve.

No. 145. Perniciotti alla Gastalda (Partridges)

Ingredients: Partridges, cauliflower, bacon, sausage, fowls' livers, carrots, onions herbs, stock, gravy, butter, Madeira.

Cut a cauliflower into quarters, blanch for a few minutes, drain, and put it into a saucepan with some bits of bacon. Let it drain on paper till dry, then arrange the bits in a circle in a deep stewpan, and in the centre put a small bit of sausage, the livers of the partridges, a fowl's liver cut up, a carrot, an onion, and a bunch of herbs. Cover about three-quarters high with good stock and gravy, put butter on the top and boil gently for an hour; then take out the sausage, replace it by two or three partridges, and simmer for three-quarters of an hour. In the meantime cut a sausage in thin slices and line a mould with it. When the birds are cooked, take them out, drain and cut them up, and fill the mould with alternate layers of partridge and cauliflower, and steam for half an hour. Five minutes before serving turn the mould over on a plate, but do not take it off, so as to let all the grease drain off. Cut up the fowls' and partridges' livers, make them into scallops and glaze them. Wipe off all the grease round the mould; take it off, garnish the dish with the scallops of liver and serve hot with an Espagnole sauce (No. 1) reduced, and add a glass of Madeira or Marsala, and a glass of essence of game to it. This is an excellent way of cooking an old partridge or pheasant.

No. 146. Beccaccini alla Diplomatica (Snipe)

Ingredients: Snipe, ham, larding bacon, herbs, Marsala, croutons, truffles, cocks' combs, mushrooms, sweetbread, tongue.

Truss fourteen snipe and cook them in a mirepoix made with plenty of ham, fat bacon, herbs, and a wine glass of Marsala. When they are cooked pour off the sauce, skim off the grease and reduce it. Take the two smallest snipe and make a forcemeat of them by pounding them in a mortar with the livers of all the snipe, then dilute this with reduced Espagnole sauce (No. 1) and add it to the first sauce. Cut twelve croutons of bread just large enough to hold a snipe each, and fry them in butter. Add some chopped herbs and truffles to the forcemeat, spread it on the croutons, and on each place a snipe and cover it with a bit of fat bacon and buttered paper. Put them in a moderate oven for a few minutes, arrange them on a dish, and pour some of their own sauce over them. Garnish the spaces between the croutons with white cocks' combs, mushrooms, and truffles. The truffles should be scooped out and filled with a little stuffing of sweetbread, tongue, and truffles mixed with a little of the sauce of the snipe. Serve the rest of the sauce in a sauce-boat.

No. 147. Piccioni alla minute (Pigeons)

Ingredients: Pigeons, butter, truffles, herbs, fowls' livers, sweetbread, salt, flour, stock, Burgundy.

Prepare two pigeons and put them into a stewpan with two ounces of butter, two truffles cut up, two fowls' livers, half-pound of sweetbread cuttings (boiled), a bunch of herbs and salt. Let them brown a little, then add a dessert-spoonful of flour mixed with stock, and half a glass of Burgundy, and stew gently for half an hour.

No. 148. Piccioni in Ripieno (Stuffed Pigeons)

Ingredients: Pigeons, sweetbread, parsley, onions, carrots, salt, pepper, bacon, stock, Chablis, fowls' livers, and gizzards.

Cut up a sweetbread, a fowl's liver and gizzard, an onion, a sprig of parsley, and add salt and pepper. Put this stuffing into two pigeons, tie larding bacon over them, and put them into a stewpan with a glass of Chablis, a cup of stock, an onion, and a carrot. When cooked pass the sauce through a sieve, skim it, add a little more sauce, and pour it over the pigeons.

No. 149. Lepre in istufato (Stewed Hare)

Ingredients: Hare, butter, onions, garlic, marjoram, celery, ham, salt, Chablis, stock, mushrooms, spice, tomatoes.

Put into a stewpan three ounces of butter, an onion cut up, a clove of garlic with a cut across it, a sprig of marjoram, and a little cut-up ham. Fry these slightly, put the hare cut up into the same stewpan, and let it get brown. Then pour a glass of Chablis and a glass of stock over it; add a little tomato sauce or a mashed-up tomato, a pinch of spice, and a few mushrooms; take out the garlic and let the rest stew gently for an hour or more. Keep the cover on the stewpan, but stir the stew occasionally.

No. 150. Lepre Agro-dolce (Hare)

Ingredients: Hare, vinegar butter, onion, ham, stock salt, sugar, chocolate, almonds, raisins.

Cut up a hare and wash the pieces in vinegar, then cook them in butter, chopped onion, some bits of ham stock and a little salt. Half fill a wine-glass with sugar and add vinegar until the glass is three-quarters full mix the vinegar and sugar well together, and when the hare is browned all over and nearly cooked, pour the vinegar over it and add a dessert spoonful of grated chocolate a few shredded almonds and stoned raisins. Mix all well together and cook for a few minutes more. This is a favourite Roman dish.

No. 151. Coniglio alla Provenzale (Rabbit)

Ingredients: Rabbit, flour butter, stock, Chablis, parsley onion, spice, mushrooms.

Cut up a rabbit, wipe the pieces, flour them over, and fry them in butter until they are coloured all over. Then pour a glass of Chablis over them, add some chopped parsley, half an onion, three mushrooms, salt, and a cup of good stock. Cover the stewpan and cook on a moderate fire for about three-quarters of an hour. Should the stew act too dry, add a spoonful of stock occasionally.

No. 152. Coniglio arrostito alla Corradino (Roast Rabbit)

Ingredients: Rabbit, pig's fry, butter, salt, pepper, fennel, bay leaf, onions.

Make a stuffing of pig's fry (previously cooked in butter), salt, pepper, fennel, an onion, all chopped up, and a bay leaf. With this stuff a rabbit well and braize it for half an hour, then roast it before a brisk fire and baste it well with good gravy. If you like, put in a clove of garlic with one cut whilst it is being braized, but only leave it in for five minutes. Serve with ham sauce (Salsa di prosciutto, No. 7.) A fowl may be cooked in this way.

No. 153. Coniglio in salsa Piccante (Rabbit)

Ingredients: Rabbit, butter, flour, celery, parsley, onion, carrot, mushrooms, cloves, spices, Burgundy, stock, capers, anchovies.

Cut up a rabbit, wipe the pieces well on a dishcloth, flour them over and put them into a frying-pan with two ounces of butter and fry for about ten minutes. Then add half a stick of celery, parsley, an onion, half a carrot, and three mushrooms, all cut up, three cloves, a pinch of spice and salt, a glass of Burgundy, and the same quantity of stock; cover the stewpan and cook for half an hour, then put the pieces of rabbit into another stewpan and pass the liquor through a sieve; press it well with a wooden spoon, so as to get as much through as possible, pour this over the rabbit and add four capers and an anchovy in brine pounded in a mortar, mix all well together, let it simmer for a few minutes, then serve hot with a garnish of croutons fried in butter.

VEGETABLES

No. 154. Asparagi alla salsa Suprema (Asparagus)

Ingredients: Asparagus, butter, nutmeg, salt, supreme sauce (No. 16) gravy, lemon, Parmesan.

Cut some asparagus into pieces about an inch long and cook them in boiling water with salt, then drain and put them into a sauté pan with one and a half ounce of melted butter and sauté for a few minutes, but first add salt, a pinch of nutmeg, and a dust of grated cheese. Pour a little supreme sauce over them, and at the last add a little gravy, one ounce of fresh butter, and a squeeze of lemon juice.

No. 155. Cavoli di Bruxelles alla Savoiarda (Brussels Sprouts)

Ingredients: Brussels sprouts, butter, pepper, stock, Bechamel sauce, Parmesan, croutons.

Take off the outside leaves of half a pound of Brussels sprouts, wash and boil them in salted water. Let them get cool, drain, and put them in a pie-dish with two ounces of fresh butter, a quarter pint of very good stock, a little pepper, and a dust of grated Parmesan. When they are well glazed over, pour off the sauce, season with three tablespoonsful of boiling Bechamel sauce (No. 3), and serve with croutons fried in butter.

No. 156. Barbabietola alla Parmigiana (Beetroot)

Ingredients: Beetroot, white sauce, Parmesan, Cheddar.

Boil a beetroot till it is quite tender, peel it, cut into slices, put it in a fireproof dish, and cover it with a thick white sauce. Strew a little grated Parmesan and Cheddar over it. Put it in the oven for a few minutes, and serve very hot in the dish.

By Urbano De Luca

No. 157. Fave alla Savoiarda (Beans)

Ingredients: Beans, stock, a bunch of herbs, Bechamel sauce.

Boil one pound of broad beans in salt and water, skin and cook them in a saucepan with a quarter pint of reduced stock and a hunch of herbs. Drain them, take out the herbs, and season with two glasses of Bechamel sauce (No. 3).

No. 158. Verze alla Capuccina (Cabbage)

Ingredients: Cabbage or greens, anchovies, salt, butter, parsley, gravy, Parmesan.

Boil two cabbages in a good deal of water, and cut them into quarters. Fry two anchovies slightly in butter and chopped parsley, add the cabbages, and at the last three tablespoonsful of good gravy, two tablespoonsful of grated Parmesan, salt and pepper, and when cooked, serve.

No. 159. Cavoli fiodi alla Lionese (Cauliflower)

Ingredients: Cauliflower, butter, onions, parsley, lemon, Espagnole sauce.

Blanch a cauliflower and boil it, but not too much. Cut up a small onion, fry it slightly in butter and chopped parsley, and when it is well coloured, add the cauliflower and finish cooking it, then take it out, put it in a dish, pour a good Espagnole sauce (No. 1) over it, and add a squeeze of lemon juice.

No. 160. Cavoli fiodi fritti (Cauliflower)

Ingredients: Cauliflower or broccoli, gravy, lemon, salt, eggs, butter.

Break up a broccoli or cauliflower into little bunches, blanch them, and put them on the fire in a saucepan with good gravy for a few minutes, then marinate them with lemon juice and salt, let them get cold, egg them over, and fry in butter.

No. 161. Cauliflower alla Parmigiana

Ingredients: Cauliflower, butter, Parmesan, Cheddar, Espagnole, stock.

Boil a cauliflower in salted water, then sauté it in butter, but be careful not to cook it too much. Take it off the fire and strew grated Parmesan and Cheddar over it then put in a fireproof dish and add a good spoonful of stock and one of Espagnole (No. 1), and put it in the oven for ten minutes.

No. 162. Cavoli Fiori Ripieni

Ingredients: Cauliflower, butter, stock, forcemeat of fowl, tongue, truffles, mushrooms, parsley, Espagnole, eggs.

Break up a cauliflower into separate little bunches, blanch them, and put them in butter, and a quarter pint of reduced stock. Make a forcemeat of fowl, add bits of tongue, truffles, mushrooms, and parsley, all cut up small and mixed with butter. With this mask the pieces of cauliflower, egg and breadcrumb them, fry like croquettes, and serve with a good Espagnole sauce (No. 1).

No. 163. Sedani alla Parmigiana (Celery)

Ingredients: Celery, stock, ham, salt, pepper, Cheddar, Parmesan, butter, gravy.

Cut all the green off a head of celery, trim the rest. Cut it into pieces about four inches long, blanch and braize them in good stock, ham, salt, and pepper. When cooked, drain and arrange them on a dish, sprinkle with grated Parmesan and Cheddar, and add one and a half ounce of butter, then put them in the oven till they have taken a good colour, pour a little good gravy over them and serve.

No. 164. Sedani fritti all'Italiana (Celery)

Ingredients: Same as No. 163, eggs, bread crumbs, tomatoes.

Prepare a head of celery as above, and cut it up into equal pieces. Blanch and braize as above, and when cold egg and breadcrumb and sauté in butter. Serve with tomato sauce.

No. 165. Cetriuoli alla Parmigiana (Cucumber)

Ingredients: Cucumber, butter, cheese, gravy, salt, cayenne.

Cut a cucumber into slices about half an inch thick, boil for five minutes in salted water, drain in a sieve, and fry slightly in melted butter, then strew a little grated Parmesan over it, and add a good thick gravy, put it into the oven for ten minutes to brown, and serve as hot as possible.

No. 166. Cetriuoli alla Borghese (Cucumber)

Ingredients: Cucumber, cream, salt, Bechamel sauce, butter, Parmesan, cayenne pepper.

Cook a cucumber as in No. 165, braize it for five minutes, add to it a good rich Bechamel (No. 3), mixed with cream and grated Parmesan Spread this well over the cucumber, and put it into the oven for ten minutes keeping the rounds of cucumber separate, so as to arrange them in a circle on a very hot dish. Care should be taken not to cook the cucumber too long, or it will break in pieces and spoil the look of the dish.

No. 167. Carote al sughillo (Carrots)

Ingredients: Carrots, stock, butter, sausage, pepper.

Boil some young carrots in stock, slice them up, and put them in a stewpan with a sausage cut up; cook for quarter of an hour on a slow fire, then stir up the fire, and when the carrots and sausage are a good colour add a good Espagnole sauce (No. 1), and serve.

No. 168. Carote e piselli alla panna (Carrots and Peas)

Ingredients: Young carrots, peas, cream, salt.

Half cook equal quantities of peas and young carrots (the carrots should be cut in dice, and will require a little longer cooking), then put them together in a stewpan with three or four tablespoonsful of cream, and cook till quite tender. Serve hot.

No. 169. Verze alla Certosine (Cabbage)

Ingredients: Cabbage, butter, salt, leeks or shallots, sardines, cheese.

Any vegetable may be cooked in the following simple manner: Boil them well, then slightly fry a little bit of leek or shallot and a sardine in butter; drain the vegetables, put them in the butter, and cook gently so that they may absorb all the flavour, and at the last add a dust of grated cheese and a tiny pinch of spice.

No. 170. Lattughe al sugo (Lettuce)

Ingredients: Lettuce, Parmesan, bacon, stock, butter, croutons of bread, gravy.

Take off the outside leaves of a lettuce, blanch and drain them well. Put on each leaf a mixture of grated Parmesan, salt, little bits of chopped bacon or ham, add a little good stock, cover over with buttered paper, and cook in a hot oven for five minutes. Then drain off the stock and roll up each leaf with the bacon, &c., put them on croutons of fried bread and pour some good thick gravy over them.

By Urbano De Luca

No. 171 Lattughe farcite alla Genovese (Lettuce)

Ingredients: Lettuce, forcemeat of fowl or veal, ham, Espagnole sauce.

Prepare a lettuce as above, and spread on each leaf a spoonful of forcemeat of fowl or veal, add a little cooked ham chopped up, roll up the leaves, and cook as above. Drain them on a cloth, arrange them neatly on a dish, and pour some good Espagnole sauce (No. 1) over them.

No. 172. Funghi cappelle infarcite (Stuffed Mushrooms)

Ingredients: Mushrooms, bread, stock, garlic, parsley, salt, Parmesan, butter, eggs, cream.

Choose a dozen good fresh mushrooms, take off the stalks and put the tops into a saucepan with a little butter. See that they lie bottom upwards. Then cut up and mix together half the stalks of the mushrooms, a little bread crumb soaked in gravy, the merest scrap of garlic and a little chopped parsley. Put this into a separate saucepan and add to it two eggs, half a gill of cream, salt, and two tablespoonsful of grated Parmesan. Mix well so as to get a smooth paste and fill in the cavities of the mushrooms with it. Then add a little more butter, strew some bread crumbs over each mushroom, and cook in the oven for ten to fifteen minutes.

No. 173. Verdure miste (Macedoine of Vegetables)

Ingredients: Cauliflower, carrots, celery, spinach, butter, cream, pepper, Parmesan.

Boil some carrots, cauliflower, spinach, and celery (all cut up) in water. Then put them in layers in a buttered china mould, and between each layer add a little cream, pepper, and a little grated Parmesan and Cheddar. Fill the mould in this manner, and put it in the oven for half an hour, so that the vegetables may cook without adhering to the mould. Turn out and serve.

No. 174. Patate alla crema (Potatoes in cream)

Ingredients: Potatoes, butter, Parmesan, white stock, cream, pepper, salt.

Boil two pounds of potatoes in salted water for a quarter of an hour, peel and cut them into slices about the size of a penny, then arrange them in layers in a very deep fireproof dish (with a lid), and on each layer pour a little melted butter, a little good white stock and a dust of grated Parmesan. Reduce a pint and a half of cream to half its quantity, add a little pepper, and pour it over the potatoes. Put the dish in the oven for twenty minutes. Serve as hot as possible.

No. 175. Cestelline di patate alla giardiniera (Potatoes)

Ingredients: Potatoes, white stock, salt, butter, peas, asparagus, sprouts, beans, &c.

Choose some big sound potatoes, cut them in half and scoop out a little of the centre so as to form a cavity, blanch them in salted water and cook for a quarter of an hour in good white stock and a little butter. Then fill in the cavities with a macedoine of cooked vegetables and add a little cream to each.

No. 176. Patate al Pomidoro (Potatoes with Tomato Sauce)

Ingredients: Potatoes, butter, salt, tomatoes, lemon, stock.

Peel three or four raw potatoes, cut them in slices about the size of a five-shilling piece, then put them into a stewpan with two ounces of melted butter, and cook them gently until they are a good colour, add salt, drain off the butter, then glaze them by adding half a glass of good stock. Arrange them on a dish, pour some good tomato sauce over them, and add a little butter and a squeeze of lemon juice.

No. 177. Spinaci alla Milanese (Spinach)

Ingredients: Spinach, butter, Velute sauce, salt, pepper, flour, stock.

Wash three pounds of spinach at least six times, boil it in a pint of water, then mince it up very fine, pass it through a hair-sieve, and put it in a saucepan with one and a half ounces of butter, add a cupful of reduced Velute sauce (No. 2) with cream, salt, and pepper, add a dessert-spoonful of flour and butter mixed, and boil until the spinach is firm enough to make into a shape, garnish with hardboiled eggs cut into quarters, and pour a good Espagnole sauce (No. 1) round the dish.

No. 178. Insalata di patate (Potato salad)

Ingredients: New potatoes, oil, white vinegar, onions, parsley, tarragon, chervil, celery, cream, salt, pepper, tarragon vinegar, watercress, cucumber, truffles.

Steam as many new potatoes as you require until they are well cooked, let them get cold, cut them into slices and pour three teaspoonsful of salad oil and one of white vinegar over them. Then rub a salad bowl with onion, put in a layer of the potato slices, and sprinkle with chopped parsley, tarragon, chervil, and celery, then another layer of potatoes until you have used all the potatoes; cover them with whipped cream seasoned with salt, pepper, and a little tarragon vinegar, and garnish the top with watercress, a few thin slices of truffle cooked in white wine, and some slices of cooked cucumber.

No. 179. Insalata alla Navarino (Salad)

Ingredients: Peas, bean onions, potatoes, tarragon, chives, parsley, tomatoes, anchovies, oil, vinegar, ham.

Mix a tablespoonful of chopped parsley, a teaspoonful of chopped onion, a teaspoonful of tarragon and chopped chives with half a gill of oil and half a gill of vinegar. Put this into a salad bowl with all sorts of cooked vegetables: peas, haricot beans, small onions, and potatoes cut up, and mix them well but gently, so as not to break the vegetables. Then add two or three anchovies in oil, and on the top place three or four ripe tomatoes cut in slices. A little cooked smoked ham cut in dice added to this salad is a great improvement.

No. 180. Insalata di pomidoro (Tomato Salad)

Ingredients: Tomatoes, mayonnaise, shallot, horseradish, gherkin, anchovies, fish, cucumber, lettuce, chervil, tarragon, eggs.

Mix the following ingredients: two anchovies in oil boned and minced, a gill of mayonnaise sauce, a little grated horseradish, very little chopped shallot, a little cold salmon or trout, and a small gherkin chopped. With this mixture stuff some ripe tomatoes. Then make a good salad of endive or lettuce, a teaspoonful of chopped tarragon and chervil, season it with oil, vinegar, salt, and pepper (the proportions should be three of oil to one of vinegar), put a layer of slices of cucumber in the salad, place the tomatoes on the top of these, and decorate them with hard-boiled eggs passed through a wire sieve.

No. 181. Tartufi alla Dino (Truffles)

Ingredients: Truffles, fowl forcemeat, champagne.

Allow one truffle for each person, scoop out the inside, chop it up fine and mix with a good forcemeat of fowl. With this fill up the truffles, place a thin layer of truffle on the top of each, and cook them in champagne in a stewpan for about half an hour. Then take them out, make a rich sauce, to which add the champagne you have used and some of the chopped truffle, put the truffles in this sauce and keep hot for ten minutes. Serve in paper souffle cases.

MACARONI, RICE, POLENTA, AND OTHER ITALIAN PASTES

No. 182. Macaroni with Tomatoes

Ingredients: Macaroni, tomatoes, butter, onion, basil, pepper, salt.

Fry half an onion slightly in butter, and as soon as it is coloured add a puree of two big cooked tomatoes. Then boil quarter of a pound of macaroni separately, drain it and put it in a deep fireproof dish, add the tomato puree and three tablespoonsful of grated Parmesan and Cheddar mixed, and cook gently for a quarter of an hour before serving. This dish may be made with vermicelli, spaghetti, or any other Italian paste.

No. 183. Macaroni alla Casalinga

Ingredients: Macaroni, butter, stock, cheese, water, salt, nutmeg.

Cut up a quarter pound of macaroni in small pieces and put it in boiling salted water. When sufficiently cooked, drain and put it into a saucepan with two ounces of butter, add good gravy or stock, three tablespoonsful of grated Parmesan and Cheddar mixed, and a tiny pinch of nutmeg. Stir over a brisk fire, and serve very hot.

No. 184. Macaroni al Sughillo

Ingredients: Macaroni, stock, tomatoes, sausage, cheese.

Half cook four ounces of macaroni, drain it and put it in layers in a fireproof dish, and gradually add good beef gravy, four tablespoonsful of tomato puree, and thin slices of sausage. Sprinkle with grated Parmesan and Cheddar, and cook for about twenty minutes. Before serving pass the salamander over the top to brown the macaroni.

No. 185. Macaroni alla Livornese

Ingredients: Macaroni, mushrooms, tomatoes, Parmesan, butter, pepper, salt, milk.

Boil about four ounces of macaroni, and stew four or five mushrooms in milk with pepper and salt. Put a layer of the macaroni in a buttered fireproof dish, then a layer of tomato puree, then a layer of the mushrooms and another layer of macaroni. Dust it all over with grated Parmesan and Cheddar, put it in the oven for half an hour, and serve very hot.

No. 186. Tagliarelle and Lobster

Ingredients: Tagliarelle, lobster, cheese, butter.

Boil half a pound of tagliarelle, and cut up a quarter of a pound of lobster. Butter a fireproof dish, and strew it well with grated Parmesan and Cheddar mixed, then put in the tagliarelle and lobster in layers, and between each layer add a little butter. Strew grated cheese over the top, put it in the oven for twenty minutes, and brown the top with a salamander.

No. 187. Polenta

Polenta is made of ground Indian-corn, and may be used either as a separate dish or as a garnish for roast meat, pigeons, fowl, &c. It is made like porridge; gradually drop the meal with one hand into boiling stock or water, and stir continually with a wooden spoon with the other hand. In about a quarter of an hour it will be quite thick and smooth, then add a little butter and grated Parmesan, and one egg beaten up. Let it get cold, then put it in layers in a baking-dish, add a little butter to each layer, sprinkle with plenty of Parmesan, and bake it for about an hour in a slow oven. Serve hot.

No. 188. Polenta Pasticciata

Ingredients: Polenta, butter, cheese, mushrooms, tomatoes.

Prepare a good polenta as above, put it in layers in a fireproof dish, and add by degrees one and a half ounces of melted butter, two cooked mushrooms cut up, and two tablespoonsful of grated cheese. (If you like, you may add a good-sized tomato mashed up.) Put the dish in the oven, and before serving brown it over with salamander.

No. 189. Battuffoli

Ingredients: Polenta, onion, butter, salt, stock, Parmesan.

Make a somewhat firm polenta (No. 187) with half a pound of ground maize and a pint and a half of salted water, add a small onion cut up and fried in butter, and stir the polenta until it is sufficiently cooked. Then take it off the fire and arrange it by spoonsful in a large fireproof dish, and give each spoonful the shape and size of an egg. Place them one against the other, and when the first layer is done, pour over it some very good gravy or stock, and plenty of grated Parmesan. Arrange it thus layer by layer. Put it into the oven for twenty minutes, and serve very hot.

No. 190. Risotto all'Italiana

Ingredients: Rice, an onion, butter, stock, tomatoes, cheese.

Fry a small onion slightly in butter, then add half a pint of very good stock. Boil four ounces of rice, but do not let it get pulpy, add it to the above with three medium-sized tomatoes in a puree. Mix it all up well, add more stock, and two tablespoonsful of grated Parmesan and Cheddar mixed, and serve hot.

No. 191. Risotto alla Genovese

Ingredients: Rice, beef or veal, onions, parsley, butter, stock, Parmesan, sweetbread or sheep's brains.

Cut up a small onion and fry it slightly in butter with some chopped parsley, add to this a little veal, also chopped up, and a little suet. Cook for ten minutes and then add two ounces of rice to it. Mix all with a wooden spoon, and after a few minutes begin to add boiling stock gradually; stir with the spoon, so that the rice whilst cooking may absorb the stock; when it is half cooked add a few spoonsful of good gravy and a sweetbread or sheep's brains (previously scalded and cut up in pieces), and, if you like, a little powdered saffron dissolved in a spoonful of stock and three tablespoonsful of grated Parmesan and Cheddar mixed. Stir well until the rice is quite cooked, but take care not to get it into a pulp.

No. 192. Risotto alla Spagnuola

Ingredients: Rice, pork, ham, onions, tomatoes, butter, stock, vegetables, Parmesan.

Put a small bit of onion and an ounce of butter into a saucepan, add half a pound of tomatoes cut up and fry for a few minutes. Then put in some bits of loin of pork cut into dice and some bits of lean ham. After a time add four ounces of rice and good stock, and as soon as it begins to boil put on the cover and put the saucepan on a moderate fire. When the rice is half cooked add any sort of vegetable, by preference peas, asparagus cut up, beans, and cucumber cut up, cook for another quarter of an hour, and serve with grated Parmesan and Cheddar mixed and good gravy.

No. 193. Risotto alla Capuccina

Ingredients: Risotto (No. 190) eggs, truffles, smoked tongue, butter.

Make a good risotto, and when cooked put it into a fireproof dish. When cold cut into shapes with a dariole mould and fry for a few minutes in butter, then turn the darioles out, scoop out a little of each and fill it with eggs beaten up, cover each with a slice of truffle and garnish with a little chopped tongue. Put them in the oven for ten minutes.

No. 194. Risotto alla Parigina

Ingredients: Risotto (No. 190), game, sauce, butter.

Make a good risotto, and when cooked pour it into a fireproof dish, let it get cold, and then cut it out with a dariole mould, or else form it into little balls about the size of a pigeon's egg. Fry these in butter and serve with a rich game sauce poured over them.

No. 195. Ravioli

Ingredients: Flour, eggs, butter, salt, forcemeat, Parmesan, gravy or stock.

Make a paste with a quarter pound of flour, the yolk of two eggs, a little salt and two ounces of butter. Knead this into a firm smooth paste and wrap it up in a damp cloth for half an hour, then roll it out as thin as possible, moisten it with a paste-brush dipped in water, and cut it into circular pieces about three inches in diameter. On each piece put about a teaspoonful of forcemeat of fowl, game, or fish mixed with a little grated Parmesan and the yolks of one or two eggs. Fold the paste over the forcemeat and pinch the edges together, so as to give them the shape of little puffs; let them dry in the larder, then blanch by boiling them in stock for quarter of an hour and drain them in a napkin. Butter a fireproof dish, put in a layer of the ravioli, powder them over with grated Parmesan, then another layer of ravioli and more Parmesan. Then add enough very good gravy to cover them, put the dish in the oven for about twenty-five minutes, and serve in the dish.

No. 196. Ravioli alla Fiorentina

Ingredients: Beetroot, eggs, Parmesan, milk or cream, nutmeg, spices, salt, flour, gravy.

Wash a beetroot and boil it, and when it is sufficiently cooked throw it into cold water for a few minutes, then drain it, chop it up and add to it four eggs, one ounce of grated Parmesan, one ounce of grated

Cheddar, two and a half ounces of boiled cream or milk, a small pinch of nutmeg and a little salt. Mix all well together into a smooth firm paste, then roll into balls about the size of a walnut, flour them over well, let them dry for half an hour, then drop them very carefully one by one into boiling stock and when they float on the top take them out with a perforated ladle, put them in a deep dish, dust them over with Parmesan and pour good meat or game gravy over them.

No. 197. Gnocchi alla Romana

Ingredients: Semolina, butter, Parmesan, eggs, nutmeg, milk, cream.

Boil half a pint of milk in a saucepan, then add two ounces of butter, four ounces of semolina, two tablespoonsful of grated Parmesan, the yolks of three eggs, and a tiny pinch of nutmeg. Mix all well together, then let it cool, and spread out the paste so that it is about the thickness of a finger. Put a little butter and grated Parmesan and two tablespoonsful of cream in a fireproof dish, cut out the semolina paste with a small dariole mould and put it in the dish. Dust a little more Parmesan over it, put it in the oven for five minutes and serve in the dish.

No. 198. Gnocchi alla Lombarda

Ingredients: Potatoes, flour, salt, Parmesan and Gruyere cheese, butter, milk, eggs.

Boil two or three big potatoes, and pass them through a hair sieve, mix in two tablespoonsful of flour, an egg beaten up, and enough milk to form a rather firm paste; stir until it is quite smooth. Roll it into the shape of a German sausage, cut it into rounds about three quarters of an inch thick, and put it into the larder to dry for about half an hour. Then drop the gnocchi one by one into boiling salted water and boil for ten minutes. Take them out with a slice, and put them in a well-buttered fireproof dish, add butter between each layer, and strew plenty of grated Parmesan and Cheddar over them. Put them in the oven for ten minutes, brown the top with a salamander, and serve very hot.

No. 199. Frittata di Riso (Savoury Rice Pancake)

Ingredients: Rice, milk, salt, butter, cinnamon, eggs, Parmesan.

Boil quarter of a pound of rice in milk until it is quite soft and pulpy, drain off the milk and add to the rice an ounce of butter, two tablespoonsful of grated Parmesan, and a pinch of cinnamon, and when it has got rather cold, the yolks of four eggs beaten up. Mix all well together, and with this make a pancake with butter in a frying pan.

OMELETTES AND OTHER EGG DISHES

No. 200. Uova al Tartufi (Eggs with Truffles)

Ingredients: Eggs, butter, cream, truffles, Velute sauce, croutons.

Beat up six eggs, pass them through a sieve, and put them into a saucepan with two ounces of butter and two tablespoonsful of cream. Put the saucepan in a bain-marie, and stir so that the eggs may not adhere. Sauté some slices of truffle in butter, cover them with Velute sauce (No. 2) and a glass of Marsala, and add them to the eggs. Serve very hot with fried and glazed croutons. Instead of truffles you can use asparagus tips, peas, or cooked ham.

No. 201. Uova al Pomidoro (Eggs and Tomatoes)

Ingredients: Eggs, salt, tomatoes, onion, parsley, butter, pepper.

Cut up three or four tomatoes, and put them into a stewpan with a piece of butter the size of a walnut and a clove of garlic with a cut in it.

Put the lid on the stewpan and cook till quite soft, then take out the garlic, strain the tomatoes through a fine strainer into a bain-marie, beat up two eggs and add them to the tomatoes, and stir till quite thick, then put in two tablespoonsful of grated cheese, and serve on toast.

No. 202. Uova ripiene (Canapes of Egg)

Ingredients: Eggs, butter, salt, pepper, nutmeg, cheese, parsley, mushrooms, Bechamel and Espagnole sauce, stock.

Boil as many eggs as you want hard, and cut them in half lengthwise; take out the yolks and mix them with some fresh butter, salt, pepper, very little nutmeg, grated cheese, a little chopped parsley, and cooked mushrooms also chopped. Then mix two tablespoonsful of good Bechamel sauce (No. 3) with the raw yolk of one or two eggs and add it to the rest. Put all in a saucepan with an ounce of butter and good stock, then fill up the white halves with the mixture, giving them a good shape; heat them in a bain-marie, and serve with a very good clear Espagnole sauce (No. 1).

No. 203. Uova alla Fiorentina (Eggs)

Ingredients: Eggs, butter, Parmesan, cream, flour, salt, pepper, curds.

Boil as many eggs as you require hard, then cut them in half and take out the yolks and pound them in a mortar with equal quantities of butter and curds, a tablespoonful of grated Parmesan, salt and pepper. Put this in a saucepan and add the yolks of eight eggs and the white of one (this is for twelve people), mix all well together and reduce a little. With this mixture fill the hard whites of the eggs and spread the rest of the sauce on the bottom of the dish, and on this place the whites. Then in another saucepan mix half a gill of cream and an ounce of butter, a dessert-spoonful of flour, salt, and pepper; let this boil for a minute, and then glaze over the eggs in the dish with it, and on the top of each egg put a little bit of butter, and over all a powdering of grated cheese. Put this in the oven, pass the salamander over the top, and when the cheese is coloured serve at once.

No. 204. Uova in fili (Egg Canapes)

Ingredients: Eggs, butter, mushrooms, onions, flour, white wine, fish or meat stock, salt, pepper, croutons of bread.

Put into a saucepan two ounces of butter, three large fresh mushrooms cut into slices, and an onion cut up, fry them slightly, and when the onion begins to colour add a spoonful of flour, a quarter of a glass of Chablis, salt and pepper, and occasionally add a spoonful of either fish or meat stock. Let this simmer for half an hour, so as to reduce it to a thick sauce. Then boil as many eggs as you want hard; take out the yolks, but keep them whole. Cut up the whites into slices, and add them to the above sauce, pour the sauce into a dish, and on the top of it place the whole yolks of egg, each on a crouton of bread.

No. 205. Frittata di funghi (Mushroom Omelette)

Ingredients: Mushrooms, butter, eggs, bread crumbs, Parmesan, marjoram, garlic.

Clean four or five mushrooms, cut them up, and put them into a frying-pan with one and a half ounces of butter, a clove of garlic with two cuts in it, and a little salt; fry them lightly till the mushrooms are nearly cooked, and then take out the garlic. In the meantime beat up separately the yolks and the whites of two or three eggs, add a little crumb of bread soaked in water, a tablespoonful of grated Parmesan, and two leaves of marjoram; go on beating all up until the crumb of bread has become entirely absorbed by the eggs, then pour this mixture into the frying-pan with the mushrooms, mix all well together and make an omelette in the usual way.

No. 206. Frittata con Pomidoro (Tomato Omelette)

Ingredients: Eggs, tomatoes, butter, marjoram, parsley, spice.

Peel two tomatoes and take out the seeds; then mix them with an ounce of butter, chopped marjoram, parsley, and a tiny pinch of spice. Add three eggs beaten up (the yolks and whites separately), and make an omelette.

No. 207. Frittata con Asparagi (Asparagus Omelette)

Ingredients: Eggs, asparagus, butter, ham, herbs, cheese.

Blanch a dozen heads of asparagus and cook them slightly, then cut them up and mix with two ounces of butter, bits of cut-up ham, herbs, and a tablespoonful of grated Parmesan. Add them to three beaten-up eggs and make an omelette.

No. 208. Frittata con erbe (Omelette with Herbs)

Ingredients: Eggs, onions, sorrel, mint, parsley, asparagus, marjoram, salt, pepper, butter.

Chop a little sorrel, a small bit of onion, mint, parsley, marjoram, and fry in two ounces of butter, add some cut-up asparagus, salt, and pepper. Then add three eggs beaten up and a little grated cheese, and make your omelette.

No. 209. Frittata Montata (Omelette Souffle)

Ingredients: Eggs, Parmesan, pepper, parsley.

Beat up the whites of three eggs to a froth and the yolks separately with a tablespoonful of grated Parmesan, chopped parsley, and a little pepper. Then mix them and make a light omelette.

No. 210. Frittata di Prosciutto (Ham Omelette)

Ingredients: Eggs, ham, Parmesan, mint, pepper, clotted cream.

Beat up three eggs and add to them two tablespoonsful of clotted cream, one tablespoonful of chopped ham, one of grated Parmesan, chopped mint and a little pepper, and make the omelette in the usual way.

SWEETS AND CAKES

No. 211. Bodino of Semolina

Ingredients: Semolina, milk, eggs, castor sugar, lemon, sultanas, rum, butter, cream, or Zabajone (No. 222).

Boil one and a half pints of milk with four ounces of castor sugar, and gradually add five ounces of semolina, boil for a quarter of an hour more and stir continually with a wooden spoon, then take the saucepan off the fire, and when it is cooled a little, add the yolks of six and the whites of two eggs well beaten up, a little grated lemon peel, three-quarters of an ounce of sultanas and two small glasses of rum. Mix well, so as to get it very smooth, pour it into a buttered mould and serve either hot or cold. If cold, put whipped cream flavoured with stick vanilla round the dish; if hot, a Zabajone (No. 222).

No. 212. Crema rappresa (Coffee Cream)

Ingredients: Coffee, cream, eggs, sugar, butter.

Bruise five ounces of freshly roasted Mocha coffee, and add it to three-quarters of a pint of boiling cream; cover the saucepan, let it simmer for twenty minutes, then pass through a bit of fine muslin. In the meantime mix the yolks of ten eggs and two whole eggs with eight ounces of castor sugar and a glass of cream; add the coffee cream to this and pass the whole through a fine sieve into a buttered mould. Steam in a bain-marie for rather more than an hour, but do not let the water boil; then put the cream on ice for about an hour, and before serving turn it out on a dish and pour some cream flavoured with stick vanilla round it.

No. 213. Crema Montata alle Fragole (Strawberry Cream)

Ingredients: Cream, castor sugar, Maraschino, strawberries or strawberry jam.

Put a pint of cream on ice, and after two hours whip it up. Pass three tablespoonsful of strawberry jam through a sieve and add two tablespoonsful of Maraschino; mix this with the cream and build it up into a pyramid. Garnish with meringue biscuits and serve quickly. You may use fresh strawberries when in season, but then add castor sugar to taste.

No. 214. Croccante di Mandorle (Cream Nougat)

Ingredients: Almonds, sugar, lemon juice, butter, castor sugar, pistachios, preserved fruits.

Blanch half a pound of almonds, cut them into shreds and dry them in a slow oven until they are a light brown colour; then put a quarter pound of lump sugar into a saucepan and caramel it lightly; stir well with a wooden spoon. When the sugar is dissolved, throw the hot almonds into it and also a little lemon juice. Take the saucepan off the fire and mix the almonds with the sugar, pour it into a buttered mould and press it against the sides of the mould with a lemon, but remember that the casing of sugar must be very thin. (You may, if you like, spread out the mixture on a flat dish and line the mould with your hands, but the sugar must be kept hot.) Then take it out of the mould and decorate it with castor sugar, pistacchio nuts, and preserved fruits. Fill this case with whipped cream and preserved fruits or fresh strawberries.

No. 215. Crema tartara alla Caramella (Caramel Cream)

Ingredients: Cream, eggs, caramel sugar, vanilla or lemon flavouring.

Boil a pint of cream and give it any flavour you like. When cold, add the yolks of eight eggs and two tablespoonsful of castor sugar, mix well and pass it through a sieve; then burn some sugar to a caramel, line a smooth mould with it and pour the cream into it. Boil in a bain-marie for an hour and serve hot or cold.

No. 216. Cremona Cake

Ingredients: Ground rice, ground maize, sugar, one orange, eggs, salt, cream, Maraschino, almonds, preserved cherries.

Weigh three eggs, and take equal quantities of castor sugar, butter, ground rice and maize (the last two together); make a light paste with them, but only use one whole egg and the yolks of the two others, add the scraped peel of an orange and a pinch of salt. Roll this paste out to the thickness of a five-shilling piece, colour it with the yolk of an egg and bake it in a cake tin in a hot oven until it is a good colour, then take it out and cut it into four equal circular pieces. Have ready some well-whipped cream and flavour it with Maraschino, put a thick layer of this on one of the rounds of pastry, then cover it with: the next round, on which also put a layer of cream, and so on until you come to the last round, which forms the top of the cake. Then split some almonds and colour them in the oven, cover the top of the cake with icing sugar flavoured with orange, and decorate the top with the almonds and preserved cherries.

No. 217. Cake alla Tolentina

Ingredients: Sponge-cake, jam, brandy or Maraschino, cream, pine-apple.

Make a medium-sized sponge-cake; when cold cut off the top and scoop out all the middle and leave only the brown case; cover the outside with a good coating of jam or red currant jelly, and decorate it with some of the white of the cake cut into fancy shapes. Soak the rest of the crumb in brandy or Maraschino and mix it with quarter of a pint of whipped cream and bits of pineapple cut into small dice; fill the cake with this; pile it up high in the centre and decorate the top with the brown top cut into fancy shapes.

No. 218. Riso all'Imperatrice

Ingredients: Rice, sugar, milk, ice, preserved fruits, blanc-mange, Maraschino, cream.

Boil two dessert-spoonsful of rice and one of sugar in milk. When sufficiently boiled, drain the rice and let it get cold. In the meantime place a mould on ice, and decorate it with slices of preserved fruit, and fix them to the mould with just enough nearly cold dissolved isinglass to keep them in place. Also put half a pint of blanc-mange on the ice, and stir it till it is the right consistency, gradually add the boiled rice, half a glass of Maraschino, some bits of pineapple cut in dice, and last of all half a pint of whipped cream. Fill the mould with this, and when it is sufficiently cold, turn it out and serve with a garnish of glace fruits or a few brandy cherries.

No. 219. Amaretti leggieri (Almond Cakes)

Ingredients: Almonds (sweet and bitter), eggs, castor sugar.

Blanch equal quantities of sweet and bitter almonds, and dry them a little in the oven, then pound them in a mortar, and add nearly double their quantity of castor sugar. Mix with the white of an egg well beaten up into a snow, and shape into little balls about the size of a pigeon's egg. Put them on a piece of stout white paper, and bake them in a very slow oven. They should be very light and delicate in flavour.

No. 220. Cakes alla Livornese

Ingredients: Almonds, eggs, sugar, salt, potato flour, butter.

Pound two ounces of almonds, and mix them with the yolks of two eggs and a spoonful of castor sugar flavoured with orange juice. Then mix two ounces of sugar with an egg, and to this add the almonds, a pinch of salt, and gradually strew in one and a half ounces of potato flour. When it is all well mixed, add one ounce of melted butter, shape the cakes and bake them in a slow oven.

No. 221. Genoese Pastry

Ingredients: Eggs, sugar, butter, flour, almonds, orange or lemon, brandy.

Weigh four eggs, and take equal weights of castor sugar, butter, and flour. Pound three ounces of almonds, and mix them with an egg, melt the butter, and mix all the ingredients with a wooden spoon in a pudding basin for ten minutes, then add a little scraped orange or lemon peel, and a dessert-spoonful of brandy. Spread out the paste in thin layers on a copper baking sheet, cover them with buttered paper, and bake in a moderately hot oven.

These cakes must be cut into shapes when they are hot, as otherwise they will break.

No. 222. Zabajone

Ingredients: Eggs, sugar, Marsala, Maraschino or other light-coloured liqueur, sponge fingers.

Zabajone is a kind of syllabub. It is made with Marsala and Maraschino, or Marsala and yellow Chartreuse. Reckon the quantities as follows: for each person the yolks of three eggs, one teaspoonful of castor sugar to each egg, and a wine-glass of wine and liqueur mixed. Whip up the yolks of the eggs with the sugar, then gradually add the wine. Put this in a bain-marie, and stir until it has thickened to the consistency of a custard. Take care, however, that it does not boil. Serve hot in custard glasses, and hand sponge fingers with it.

No. 223. Iced Zabajone

Ingredients: Eggs, castor sugar, Marsala, cinnamon, lemon, stick vanilla, rum, Maraschino, butter, ice.

Mix the yolks of ten eggs, two dessert-spoonsful of castor sugar, and three wine-glasses of Marsala, add half a stick of vanilla, a small bit of whole cinnamon, and the peel of half a lemon cut into slices.

Whip this up lightly over a slow fire until it is nearly boiling and slightly frothy; then remove it, take out the cinnamon, vanilla, and lemon pool, and whip up the rest for a minute or two away from the fire. Add a tablespoonful of Maraschino and one of rum, and, if you like, a small quantity of dissolved isinglass. Stir up the whole, pour it into a silver souffle dish, and put it on ice. Serve with sponge cakes or iced wafers.

No. 224. Pan-forte di Siena (Sienese Hardbake)

Ingredients: Honey, almonds, filberts, candied lemon peel, pepper, cinnamon, chocolate, corn flour, large wafers.

Boil half a pound of honey in a copper vessel, and then add to it a few blanched almonds and filberts cut in halves or quarters and slightly browned, a little candied lemon peel, a dust of pepper and powdered cinnamon and a quarter pound of grated chocolate. Mix all well together, and gradually add a tablespoonful of corn flour end two of ground almonds to thicken it. Then take the vessel off the fire, spread the mixture on large wafers, and make each cake about an inch thick. Garnish them on the top with almonds cut in half, and dust over a little powdered sugar and cinnamon, then put them in a very slow oven for an hour.

No. 225. Fish Sauce

Add one dessert-spoonful of New Century Sauce sauce to a quarter pint of melted butter sauce.

No. 226. Sauce Piquante (for Meat, Fowl, Game, Rabbit, &c.)

One dessert-spoonful to a quarter pint of ordinary brown or white stock. It may be thickened by a roux made by frying two ounces of butter with two ounces of flour.

No. 227. Sauce for Venison, Hare, &c.

Two dessert-spoonsful of New Century Sauce to half a pint of game gravy or sauce, and a small teaspoonful of red currant jelly.

No. 228. Tomato Sauce Piquante

Fry three medium-sized tomatoes in one and a half ounce of butter. Pass this through a sieve, then boil it up in a bain-marie till it thickens, and add one dessertspoonful of New Century Sauce.

No. 229. Sauce for Roast Pork, Ham, &c.

Add to any ordinary white or brown sauce one dessert-spoonful of New Century Sauce and two of port or Burgundy if the sauce is brown, two of Chablis if white.

No. 230. For masking Cutlets, &c.

Making a roux by frying two ounces of butter with two ounces of flour, and add two tablespoonsful of boiling stock. Stir in one dessert-spoonful of New Century Sauce. Let it get cold, and it will then be quite firm and ready for masking cutlets, &c.

Essentials of Classic Italian Cooking

By Urbano De Luca

www.ingramcontent.com/pod-product-compliance
Lightning Source LLC
Chambersburg PA
CBHW081625100526
44590CB00021B/3602